KAIZEN TEIAN 1

KAIZEN TEIAN 1

Developing Systems for Continuous Improvement Through Employee Suggestions

Edited by the Japan Human Relations Association

Foreword by
Peter B. Grazier

Publisher's Message by
Norman Bodek
President, Productivity, Inc.

Productivity Press

Cambridge, Massachusetts   Norwalk, Connecticut

Originally published by Nikkan Kogyo Shimbun, Ltd., Tokyo. Copyright ©
1989 Nikkan Kogyo Shimbun, Ltd. Translated into English by Productivity
Press, Inc. Translated by Steve Vitek.

Edited by the Japan Human Relations Association
    Text of Parts 1, 2, & 3 by Bunji Tozawa, Managing Editor, JHRA
    Illustrations and cartoons by Kiyonori Kuriki, Akiko Yamamoto, Misako
        Fukui, and Mio Asahi

Productivity Press
P.O. Box 3007
Cambridge, Massachusetts 02140
Telephone: (617) 497-5146
Telefax: (617) 868-3524

Cover design by Joyce C. Weston
Printed and bound by BookCrafters
Printed in the United States of America

Library of Congress Cataloging-in-Publication Data

Kaizen teian. 1. English.
    Developing systems for continuous improvement through employee
suggestions / edited by the Japan Human Relations Association; foreword
by Peter B. Grazier.
        p. cm.
Includes index.
ISBN 0-915299-89-5
    1. Suggestion systems. I. Nihon H R Kyōkai. II. Title.
HF5549.5.S8K3513 1992
658.3'14--dc20
                                                            91-26612
                                                               CIP

93 94 10 9 8 7 6 5 4 3

Contents

Publisher's Message

What do you think of when you think of employee involvement? Every day, millions of people arrive on the job at factories, offices, and shops. They do their jobs and work hard at them — but involvement is not the same as "working hard." In too many cases, it is as if there were signs posted over the entrances of our workplaces that read, "Stifle intelligence upon entering." Workers are seen as expendable resources brought in to do the required tasks; rarely are they asked to use their brains to improve the work.

Involvement really represents a new dimension in working. People are truly involved only when they have a creative contribution to make in doing their work and in finding ways to do it better. The job itself may bring us the physical security and sense of social belonging that Maslow documented as among our basic needs. To fulfill our higher needs for recognition and self-development, however, each of us needs opportunities to share our creativity and intelligence.

A participative suggestion system is an excellent method for providing creative opportunities on a daily basis; this book, *Kaizen Teian 1*, describes in detail the reasons for using this kind of system to build involvement. *Kaizen* is a Japanese word that has become part of the language in many Western companies; it means continuous incremental improvement of the standard way of work. This kind of creative improvement is something that every employee is capable of participating in — in fact, since a front-line employee is most familiar with the actual work, there is no better person to ask for improvement ideas.

The word *teian* means proposal or suggestion. Kaizen teian — a companywide system for employee continuous improvement proposals — is one of the most effective and widespread forms of kaizen activities in Japan. It is an organized way of bringing forth the ideas of each employee, no matter how small.

This book presents convincing reasons for using the Japanese-style improvement proposal system with your company. The kaizen teian system is a different breed from the typical Western-style suggestion system, and therein lies its strength. The traditional suggestion system in the West emphasizes "few" and "big": a few people get big rewards for a few big ideas that save big bucks. Kaizen teian is not concerned with bigness so much as with broadness. It encourages the creative participation of each person in the company, drawing on the cumulative effect of many small ideas. It is a simple system that provides for quick and ongoing feedback from a person's direct supervisor about ideas submitted; in contrast, its monetary awards to employees are modest.

Kaizen Teian 1 describes another feature that distinguishes this improvement proposal system: its focus on implementation. In a typical Western system, employees deposit their ideas in a suggestion box — and wait to hear something back from the corporate suggestion committee. Since these systems often allow people to submit vague complaints or suggestions for other departments, many suggestions stall when it comes to bringing about some actual response. The natural dissatisfaction when nothing comes of an idea discourages employees from participating in the future and is a common reason behind the failure of Western suggestion systems.

The beauty of kaizen teian is that it is, in effect, a system of "walking suggestion boxes." Supervisors actively ask their employees for ideas about improving the work that they do together. Their role is to coach employees on improvement principles and methods and to teach them the skills they need to implement their proposals. Since the focus is on improving one's own processes, proposed improvements are much more likely to be within the employee's range of ability. Implemented results breed enthusiasm about contributing more ideas.

Kaizen Teian 1 provides support for managers who wish to introduce a kaizen teian system, offering examples and illustrations to describe its cycle of activities. To ensure prompt evaluation and feedback on proposals, it is important to devise a simple system with guidelines that are easy for supervisors to follow. The book presents a quick evaluation chart to serve as a model in developing your own evaluation system. Examples of simple proposal forms are also provided.

Part Four of the book includes case studies from the experience of people in organizations that use kaizen teian. Examples from an automobile plant, a department store, a bank, and a post office describe creative solutions to challenging problems in a variety of industries. These cases and the discussion questions at the end of each chapter are opportunities for discovering how you can adapt and apply these ideas to your own workplace.

Managers often have questions about the kaizen teian system; typical ones include why it's important to physically write up a proposal and whether continuous improvement should be rewarded as something different from the regular work. Chapter 6 offers explanations for these and other questions that can help pave the way for the introduction of a program.

We are pleased to bring you this book as the first volume of a three-part series on managing the kaizen teian system. *Kaizen Teian 2: Guiding Continuous Improvement Through Employee Suggestions* draws on illustrated examples to teach the basic principles of kaizen; it also expands on the use of an improvement proposal system as an OJT and skill-development method between supervisors and employees. *Kaizen Teian 3: Sustaining Continuous Improvement Through Employee Suggestions* presents the natural evolution of the proposal system into a "kaizen reporting system," which focuses implemented ideas submitted after the fact.

The material in these books was developed by Bunji Tozawa, managing editor with the Japan Human Relations Association (JHRA). Mr. Tozawa is a world-class expert in the kaizen teian system. He compiled the material that many of you know as *The Idea Book*, and has worked tirelessly to evolve the continuous improvement proposal system into the management process described in these books. In addition to writing and editing JHRA's monthly magazine, *Ingenuity and Inventions*, Mr. Tozawa also lectures and presents workshops in the United States and Europe as well as in Japan. We greatly appreciate his assistance, and that of Kenjiro Yamada, managing director of JHRA, in bringing about this translation.

Our thanks go to Peter B. Grazier, president of Teambuilding, Inc. and the author of *Before It's Too Late* for contributing a foreword to this book. Special recognition is due Mugi Hanao for assistance in clarifying the translation. Dorothy Lohmann managed the editorial preparation, with the assistance of Maureen Murray and Laura St. Clair (word processing), Christine Carvajal (manuscript editing), and Jennifer Cross (indexing). Production was managed by Gayle Joyce, assisted by Michele Saar, Karla Tolbert, and Jane Worcester. The cover was designed by Joyce C. Weston.

Norman Bodek
President
Productivity, Inc.

Karen R. Jones
TEI Series Editor
Productivity Press

Foreword

Today it is recognized in the West that to compete effectively in a global marketplace, an organization must elicit a commitment from every employee to contribute to ongoing improvement. One form of contribution is employee ideas or suggestions, and many organizations in the United States have been using traditional suggestion systems for years.

But when you look at the results, with rare exceptions the participation rate of American workers is very low. Workers in the United States submit an average of 0.2 ideas per year for improvement, compared with an average of 20 ideas per year from Japanese workers. Toyota, for example, receives over *two million* ideas each year from its workforce and implements more than 80 percent of them.

This level of participation is virtually unheard of in America, and accordingly, we question if this is really possible. *Kaizen Teian 1* shows not only that it is possible, but how Japanese organizations garner such levels of participation from their people. The book explains clearly the philosophical differences between Japanese and Western suggestion systems that make these results possible and significantly challenges our existing paradigms of the Western-style system. For example:

- Traditional Western suggestion systems typically emphasize and reward the *big idea*, whereas the Japanese system focuses on *participation*. The greater the participation, they believe, the greater the opportunity for *continual and gradual accumulation of small improvements* (kaizen).
- Western suggestion systems typically use large cash rewards to encourage participation, whereas the Japanese give smaller token amounts. The emphasis is on *contribution to the improvement and well-being of the organization*, rather than on financial rewards.
- Western suggestion systems typically are hierarchical in control and approval, while the Japanese give authority for approval and implementation to the front lines. *The best suggestion*, they believe, *is an implemented one*, and the key to implementation is in educating and empowering the front lines to control the process.

These notions challenge us to reshape our thinking about participation and innovation. Encouraging a larger segment of our workforce to contribute on an ongoing basis engenders higher levels of commitment to the organization and its mission. It fosters efforts to challenge the status quo and legitimizes the pursuit of ongoing improvements at the work station.

At a time when most quality and participation initiatives in the West are floundering, it is critical that we rethink our existing assumptions. *Kaizen Teian 1* gives us valuable insights into how we might make such changes.

Peter B. Grazier
President
Teambuilding, Inc.

Preface

The main theme of this book can be summarized in the following few words: "Ideas are valuable only if they can be implemented." Proposals that either are not implemented or cannot be implemented are like castles in the air — of no practical use.

Although a proposal system in which opinions of company employees are gathered sounds like a good idea, such a system does not make sense unless these opinions serve as a basis for action. Indeed, it is better to have no system than a pro forma proposal system only. Even more important, traditional methods of gathering opinions and ideas, such as the "suggestion box" method, are today hopelessly obsolete.

The main trend in proposal activity today is innovations and methods to implement them. Workers are cooperating in the creation of companywide, "knowledge-oriented" systems in which decisions are made quickly and innovative proposals are implemented promptly.

The question of motivation is brought up frequently in this book. If we authors sound a trifle argumentative, it is because we believe that in order to promote a bottom-up activity, which is how you can characterize innovative proposal making, you must constantly ask yourself about the motivation behind an idea or the purpose it will serve. The idea itself, without the answers to these questions, is not enough.

We want to promote a bottom-up activity that helps to develop motivation and creativity in all members of an organization. If activity is limited to a select group of employees who have little interaction with other workers, then it would be better to do nothing at all. Such half-measures serve only to weaken overall motivation and inspire distrust about the fate of the company.

We at the Japan Human Relations Association (JHRA) want to promote activity that generates innovative proposals. At the same time, we wish to discourage the type of thinking that focuses on the "other company's" way of doing things or that emphasizes technique over purpose — the *how* over the *why*. Technique alone is insufficient to power a process that unfolds "organically," from the bottom up. Too many unforeseen circumstances occur, each requiring different responses. Only by understanding the purpose of the process — the *why* — can you develop the appropriate technique.

Thus, we dedicate Volume 1 of *Kaizen Teian* to the *why* behind the continuous improvement proposal system. Volume 2 deals with the *how* of such a system: it contains accounts of numerous practical examples of innovative activity. Volume 3 gives methods for keeping a proposal system vital as it matures.

PART ONE

Introducing Kaizen
and Teian

What is the continuous improvement process we call *kaizen*? And what is a *teian* proposal system? In this part of the book we consider the concepts and mechanisms behind these terms, which are becoming known around the world.

1

What Is *Kaizen*?

In November 1986, Masaaki Imai published a book in English called *Kaizen*.* Western readers must have been somewhat taken aback by this strange word. Nevertheless, it has had a major impact on business and management worldwide. Although the notion of kaizen has been explained from many angles and used in all kinds of experimental projects, it is difficult to express this central concept of Japanese-style management clearly in just a few words.

On the other hand, the real impact was not caused by the book. Once progressive corporate managers and management consultants understood the universal character of the kaizen concept, which until then had been commonly used only by the Japanese and in Japanese companies, the concept had an enormous influence on their thinking. This is why kaizen is no longer explained as a "Japanese management concept," but rather as a new management concept that is now used and has been universally accepted all over the world. Kaizen has joined the worldwide vocabulary, together with other Japanese words

---

* Masaaki Imai, *Kaizen: The Key to Japan's Competitive Success* (New York: McGraw-Hill, 1986).

like Zen, karate, sushi, or tempura. In the past most of these adopted words came from culture, art, or cuisine; as Japanese economic and production management techniques continue to attract global attention, words from these areas are also being accepted outside Japan.

KAIZEN IS MORE THAN SIMPLY "IMPROVEMENT"

According to Masaaki Imai, kaizen means improvement, particularly continuous improvement.* Kaizen improvement is quite different from innovation, the sort of improvement with which many Westerners are more familiar.

Innovation implies significant, breakthrough-level progress by only a limited number of trained professionals such as engineers or managers. Kaizen improvement, on the other hand, means a continual and gradual accumulation of small improvements made by all employees (including executives and managers).

Japanese people have a sense of the word *kaizen* as a symbol containing all the daily struggles on the job, and the way we try to deal with them. That is why Toyota, Mazda, and other companies with plants outside Japan consciously use the Japanese word *kaizen* in their education and training for employees from overseas plants. They probably do this to clarify the distinction between kaizen improvement and innovation, and to reinforce the kaizen way of thinking about improvement.

The concept of kaizen and the managerial technique behind it is being accepted gradually in non-Japanese companies as well. In some Western plants, it is even used as a verb; employees speak of "kaizening" a process. This adoption is a sign that kaizen has now become a completely "English" word.

Generally speaking, when a new concept and way of thinking is accepted even when there are no words to accurately

---

* Imai, op. cit., p. xx.

express the concept during the process of acceptance and com-
prehension of it, such an acceptance leads to misunderstandings
and creates confusion. But once a key word is incorporated into
another language, it will become further naturalized and at
some point may be used by the general public. Judging from
history, the word *kaizen*, which is at the moment applied to a
unique method of management, may be entering a new period
in which it will be used universally and on a global scale.

Let's think carefully about what kaizen really means. We
will look at several analogies that shed light on this important
concept.

KAIZEN IS EVERY EMPLOYEE'S JOB

Every job has two important components. One of them is
maintenance, or support of the daily status quo, and the other is
destroying the status quo to improve the circumstances.*

---

* The concepts and illustrations in this section were adapted in part from
  materials appearing in Masaaki Imai, op. cit., pp. 5-7.

Maintenance means maintaining present standards and levels, the present character of the work, and so on. It consists of a very clear stipulation of standard operating procedure: the set goals and the method that should be used to achieve those goals. Only if everyone meticulously maintains all the standards will the company be able to deliver high-quality products according to its agreements, and to deliver them at the right price, within the delivery period, and with the service that is required. The confidence of the customers depends on such maintenance.

But maintenance is not the only essential component in the overall structure of a company. Also needed is a certain destructive element, an element of elimination. It is crucial to incorporate into the structure a means for breaking away from the existing circumstances so that the company can surpass present performance levels and not remain in a rut.

Everything in this world is in constant flux; nothing is permanently stable and unchangeable. If a company in this day and age cannot accommodate change, it will be left behind. In particular, if a company is unable to respond quickly to changes affecting areas of competition, competing companies, and its customers, it will soon lose its markets.

Figure 1 on page 7 shows the relationship between the maintenance and destruction of existing circumstances as they are reflected in the company hierarchy. Generally, the higher a person's position in the organization, the more weight he or she can throw around to make big changes in the present condition. In this sense, the main task of those at the top levels is to take care of the future.

By contrast, employees who have recently joined a company, temporary workers, and part-time employees must obey the instructions of their supervisors, follow the procedures in their manuals, and carry out designated tasks in a prescribed manner that must be strictly adhered to. This "maintenance" work is their most important task.

But aren't these workers capable of doing more than simply learning their jobs and following instructions? Couldn't they also have input into ways to destroy existing circumstances? For them, this could mean devising methods that are better than those currently used, bringing forth proposals, testing them, and seeking advice from other employees.

In Japanese thinking, the destruction of the present circumstances occurs on two general levels. One of them is kaizen, or continuous improvement, and the other is innovation.

Figure 1

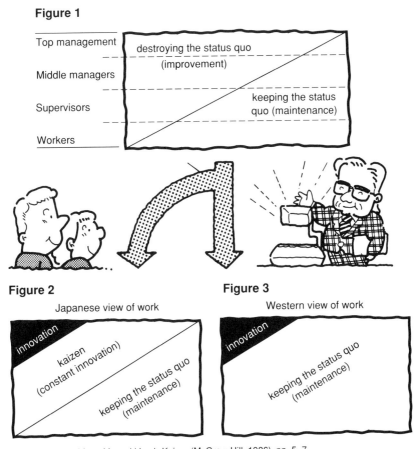

Figure 2

Japanese view of work

Figure 3

Western view of work

Source: Adapted from Masaaki Imai, *Kaizen* (McGraw-Hill, 1986), pp. 5, 7.

Generally speaking, the more authority you have and the greater your responsibility, or more specifically, the higher is your ranking in the company, the greater is your ability to effect innovation, or large-scale change in the company. Furthermore, any innovations you do make are apt to carry a significant impact and come invested with high expectations. This is not to say that the only job of top managers is to grapple with innovations, but it is certainly one of their important jobs.

Kaizen (continuous improvement), on the other hand, is a key responsibility of lower level employees. While a major innovation often requires an enormous investment and special technology, kaizen normally requires only common sense and the ability to do a job well — something that anyone is capable of.

From a Japanese perspective, successful companies are those that are able to strike an effective balance between the element of maintenance and the destructive force represented by innovations and kaizen (continuous improvement). Figure 2 illustrates this concept. As this figure shows, while only some employees participate in major innovations, all employees can participate in kaizen.

Figure 3 illustrates a typical Western view of the workplace. The notion of continuous improvement is generally lacking in this environment. "Destroying the status quo" is left primarily to an elite corps of technical workers, who are actively involved in innovation of new products, processes, and so on. The remaining employees are required only to perform their jobs according to standardized procedures described in manuals and are not asked to think about innovation at all.

KAIZEN AND INNOVATION

As we have just seen, there are two methods through which you can destroy existing conditions, achieve progress, and promote new development. One of them is innovation, and the other one is kaizen (continuous improvement). These two

methods are like a staircase versus a path leading up a hill.*
The tortoise and the hare fable from Aesop is an apt analogy.

Through innovation, a company makes dramatic progress, like a hare leaping up a staircase; through kaizen, its
progress is more like that of the tortoise, climbing up a path
slowly but steadily.

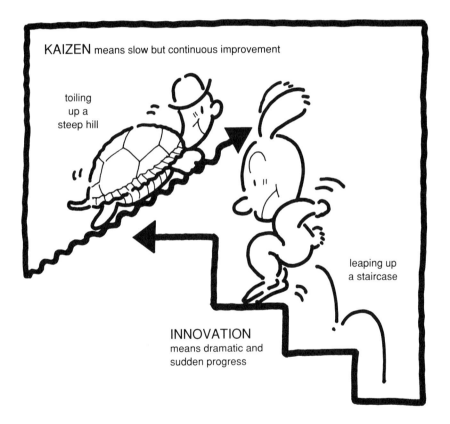

Source: Adapted from Masaaki Imai, *Kaizen* (McGraw-Hill, 1986), p. 25.

---

* The concepts and illustrations in this section were adapted in part from
  materials appearing in Masaaki Imai, op. cit., pp. 25-27.

Kaizen Means Everyone Is Welcome to Participate

Major innovations bring about remarkable results, but they require the spending of large sums of money and use of the best technology. They may involve development of new ways of doing business, development of new products, or large investments in equipment, expansion of sales facilities, and similar measures. It takes people of a certain ability to accomplish overwhelming results; it also takes a lot of material, money, technology, and time. Truly incredible results can be achieved in this way, but this approach also involves a considerable risk.

Not everyone can confront such momentous tasks easily. Only people who have sufficient ability and authority can be entrusted with a great deal of responsibility. They must make full use of specialized techniques and have the latest technology at their disposal.

On the other hand, kaizen, or continuous improvement, represents incremental, ongoing progress as one small invention is added to another. It may not represent major and revolutionary inventions, but it is something that everyone can participate in, using common sense to make logical improvements.

That is why the kaizen movement is promoted as an ongoing event for all employees. Since kaizen is something that everyone can do, everyone can be asked to participate. By contrast, it would be nonsense to expect all employees of a company to participate in major innovations or inventions, things that few people can handle.

If only a few isolated employees come up with small incremental innovations, modest improvement will be achieved, but major results are not possible. However, when a constant stream of small improvements flows from *all* employees of a company, a powerful force is set in motion.

Kaizen and Innovation Are Two Wheels of a Cart

Kaizen and innovation are both indispensable for a well-functioning corporation. Kaizen, or continuous improvement, alone will not give you the competitive edge over rivals who are working on new innovations. In that sense it is like a rickshaw ride; it cannot compete with a car ride, no matter how much effort you give to it.

Innovation can bring about unparalleled progress and changes that are truly revolutionary. It would be futile to resist the great changes of this era. Unless a corporation participates in this process of revolutionary change, it will be unable to transform itself as required, and it will not grow.

This is not to say that only momentous innovation will help you beat the competition. When a corporation is interested only in major innovations, it will not be able to maintain any competitive edge it gains. Clearly, a corporation can maintain momentum only if it can unleash the power hidden in the dual approach of great innovation and small incremental improvements.

Even if a great system is established through major innovation, maintaining and improving this system requires that a lot of effort be put into small continuous improvements; otherwise, the efficiency of this system will soon decline.

As soon as any system has been established, it will start deteriorating. This is the fate of all systems. Nothing in the world is immune from change. Therefore, persistence is essential to maintaining a system in good order.

Major innovations are like winning a short sprint. They represent a victory, but they alone will not ensure continuous success and results. Once complacency sets in on the inside and a competitor moves in from the outside, the effect of any major invention will soon be destroyed.

ideal level
(standard maintenance)

INNOVATION

The status quo slips when major innovations are not backed up by
kaizen improvements

Source: Adapted from Masaaki Imai, *Kaizen* (McGraw-Hill, 1986), p. 26.

If you become blinded by the success of your revolutionary innovation and neglect to make minor daily improvements, it won't be long before your shares drop in value, your reputation deteriorates, and other unfortunate consequences ensue. It is a gradual process, but in the end you will lose the race, like the foolish hare who fell asleep after gaining the lead.

On the other hand, a series of small improvements brings steady progress and results over a long period of time. That is because continuous improvements not only serve to maintain existing standards but also *raise* those standards in daily activities of people who are doing their job.

This is why, in companies where continuous improvement is common practice, "standards" are perceived as nothing more than temporary criteria, stepping-stones to a better way. A new standard, established with the help of a major innovation, can be upgraded by a series of small kaizen improvements until a qualitatively new standard is reached.

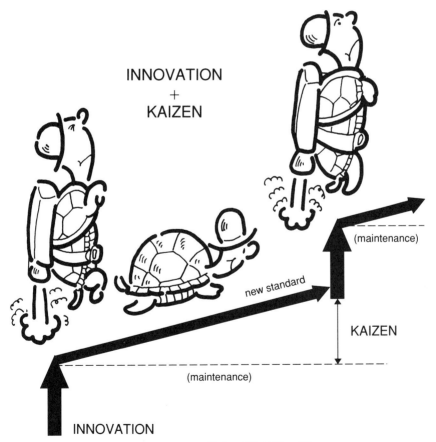

INNOVATION
+
KAIZEN

(maintenance)

new standard

KAIZEN

(maintenance)

INNOVATION

Source: Adapted from Masaaki Imai, *Kaizen* (McGraw-Hill, 1986), p. 27.

Especially if you are operating in a mature and diversified market, a major innovation alone will not make you responsive enough. When this innovation is not accompanied by kaizen improvement, when success is taken for granted and standards are not continually revised, it is impossible to provide the kind of response that is required by changing and diversified markets.

To provide the best possible service to the customer, you need to propose, evaluate, and gradually implement small improvements directly in the workplace. A nonchalant level of service, typical of systems where authority is centralized, no longer serves customer needs. Good service can be provided only when every employee has access to information and can contribute his or her own ideas at the workplace, wherever it may be. The strength of such a system lies in a series of continuous small improvements. That is why kaizen improvement systems have been completely decentralized, and why these improvements are carried out directly at the place of work.

DISCUSSION QUESTIONS

What are the two essential components of every business organization?

In Japanese terms, what are the two ways of disrupting the status quo, or making improvements, in a company?

Who has responsibility for each of these types of improvement?

Define *kaizen*.

2

What Is a *Teian* System?

PROPOSAL SYSTEMS VERSUS SUGGESTION SYSTEMS

There are big differences between the proposal system that is developing in Japan and the Western-style suggestion system. Just as the meaning of *kaizen* differs from that of *improvement*, so does the concept of *proposals* differ from the concept of *suggestions*.

Needless to say, many Japanese proposal systems introduced after World War II were systems learned from companies in the United States. In the years since, Japanese companies have devised, improved, and developed their own independent systems.

This is why there is now a big difference between the *teian* system of Japan and the suggestion system of the West. This distinction must be kept in mind, as *teian* is often translated simply as "suggestion," which tends to complicate communication with Western readers.

For example, it would be a mistake to simply compare the number of employee "suggestions" submitted in Japan and "suggestions" submitted in the United States each year, saying,

15

"Japanese companies receive many more suggestions than U.S. companies — as much as 300 times more. Judging by this, America is in bad shape." There are critical differences between the approaches used in the two countries, not only in the definitions of *proposals* and *suggestions,* but also in review and evaluation methods, amounts of awards, and the role of the system in the company management.

This is why the JHRA uses the word *teian,* or "proposal," when explaining the concepts of Japanese-style proposal activities in the seminars conducted for Western managers. Like *kaizen,* the word *teian* is gradually gaining acceptance all over the world.

A Different Motivation for Participation

How is the Japanese-style proposal different from a Western-style suggestion? One of the differences is shown in the illustration on page 17. This promotional poster from the U.S. Food and Drug Administration straightforwardly encourages people to come up with ideas, using the message "ideas pay off" and the suggestion of a personal reward. This poster accurately expresses the concept of "cash for your idea" — a businesslike transaction between the company and whoever comes up with a suggestion.

It is unlikely that you would see a similar promotional poster in Japan. Although Japanese proposal systems do pay bonuses, the financial aspect of the proposal system typically would not be stressed. Japanese posters would more likely present a different kind of appeal, such as "Let's improve the way we work," or "Let's make our company stronger." A Western worker, used to the idea that a suggestion is something that makes or saves money, might not understand how these posters would motivate someone to make improvements.

"IDEAS" PAY OFF!

SUBMIT ONE TODAY

Data Speak Louder Than Concepts

Let us take a look at the data behind the concepts we have been discussing. The chart on page 18 compares the results of a study of Japanese and U.S. proposal systems. In 1989, Japanese employees brought forward an average of 36 proposals per employee per year, while in the United States only 0.12 proposals were made per employee per year. Why was the difference so striking — approximately 300 times more in one country than in the other?

Comparison of Results of Suggestion Systems
in Japan and the United States (1989)

	United States	Japan
Number of reporting organizations	282	666
Number eligible	8,642,269	1,646,960
Total suggestions received	996,694	60,343,937
Number of suggestions/100 eligible	12	3,664
Number of employees submitting/100 eligible	9	75
Adoption rate	32%	87%
Average award payment/adoption	$602.15	$2.20 *
Average net savings/adoption	$6,114	$110 **
Net savings/100 eligible	$22,825	$365,656 ***

Notes:

Japan: Total results include private and government organizations.
  * Reflects results of 555 organizations.
  ** Reflects results of 325 organizations.
  *** Reflects results of 357 organizations.
  Calculated at an exchange rate of ¥150/$1.

Source: Research conducted by the JHRA and the National Association of Suggestion Systems (U.S.)

When we compare the 1989 figures for the amount of economic effect (profit or cost savings) realized per proposal, in Japan this amount was only $110, while in the United States it was $6,114. What is even more surprising is that Japanese companies paid an average award of $2.20 per adopted proposal, while in the United States the award per suggestion averaged $600.

To the Japanese, it is natural to accept a nominal amount of money per adopted proposal. When we talk about a proposal bonus, that is approximately the amount that comes to mind. A very good proposal can bring in much more, even several thousand yen, at the most ¥100,000 to ¥200,000 (approximately $660 to $1,300), but proposals like that are the exception rather than the rule.

That is why many Japanese are surprised to hear that the amount of a bonus per proposal in the United States averages around $600. Because of this disparity, every year people ask whether the numbers are correct. But there is no mistake in the numbers. The disparity is due to the difference between the Western-style suggestion system and the Japanese-style proposal system.

THE MECHANISM OF FINANCIAL REWARDS

Where does this difference originate? Let us start by analyzing the mechanism of award payments. The figure on page 20 shows the financial effect of a proposal in relation to award payments in Japanese and Western suggestion systems. This is expressed in terms of the reward rate — the relative return to the proposal maker for his or her idea.

The horizontal axis of this chart represents the quality of the proposals, with lower-grade proposals on the left, and the more important, highly effective proposals on the right. The vertical axis represents the increasing reward rate in terms of the amount of the award divided by the amount of the results.

In Europe and in the United States, the award payment represents approximately 10 to 20 percent of the net savings from the suggestion in one year; the illustration represents this as a fixed platform for suggestion awards.

The effect of the fixed award paid under this system also establishes the object of those payments; the object is to promote medium- or high-rated suggestions. Since lower-grade suggestions are not compensated, this is where the graph ends. This makes for a very simple and clear accounting system.

Let's compare this system with the award "picture" seen in Japanese companies. Many companies in Japan do reward proposals that would not be accepted as effective proposals, giving participation bonuses (sometimes also called proposal

The Reward Rate Mechanism

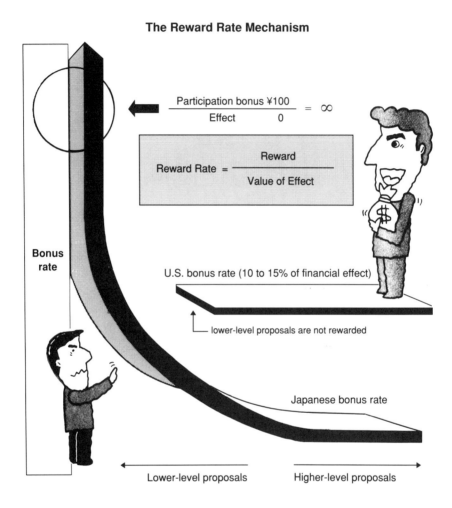

$$\frac{\text{Participation bonus } ¥100}{\text{Effect} \qquad 0} = \infty$$

$$\text{Reward Rate} = \frac{\text{Reward}}{\text{Value of Effect}}$$

Bonus rate

U.S. bonus rate (10 to 15% of financial effect)

lower-level proposals are not rewarded

Japanese bonus rate

Lower-level proposals ⟷ Higher-level proposals

bonuses) in the amount of about ¥100 to ¥300 (roughly, $.60 to $2.00). As the figure shows, even if the bonus payment is ¥1,000 (around $6.00), if that is divided by the zero financial effect of the typical proposal, the rate of reward to the proposal maker is infinitely great.

What is the situation like in the top class of proposals? Even if the resulting savings or profit achieved per proposal is tens of millions of yen or more during one year, the award will still be capped at ¥100,000 to ¥500,000 (approximately $600 to $3,000), if that much. This makes the reward rate to the proposal maker only a few percent of the financial effect. The Japanese proposal system thus gives preferential treatment to the lower levels of proposals, while not proportionately rewarding the really big ideas. The flattened-out curve on the right shows this.

However you look at it, it seems like a strange and illogical system. Nevertheless, this curve represents a typical characteristic of the kaizen teian (improvement proposal) system.

A System that Spoils Employees to Promote Participation

What is the reasoning behind the establishment of this type of system? The system was created to promote participation in proposal activity from as many employees as possible. Only an awareness of this objective can give a clear understanding of the comparative data we have just discussed.

Compared to a participation rate of 75 percent in 1989, which is typical of a Japanese proposal system, suggestion systems in the United States have a participation rate of only 9 percent. When we compare the adoption rates, it is 87 percent in Japanese companies versus 32 percent in U.S. companies. In the Japanese proposal system, most proposals will be used, will receive some kind of evaluation, and will be rewarded with some kind of a bonus. The American system is much more selective — two out of three suggestions will *not* be used.

This illustrates the fact that Western suggestion systems are designed to promote excellent, big-result ideas, which are rewarded accordingly. That is why the system does not necessarily require a large number of suggestions or a high participation rate.

In the Japanese system, on the other hand, even small proposals and ideas are welcomed and carefully collected, because even small proposals are considered to have an educational value. Each of the systems has its advantages and shortcomings.

The Japanese method creates a system that "spoils" or "pampers" employees; it can hardly be disputed that it is skewed toward rewarding employees for participation, even if a large percentage of proposals may not be useful.

In such a system, there will always be those who say: "Are these proposals written by adults or children? If this is what our company pays bonuses for, we might as well be running a kindergarten." There is a danger that such a system will create waste by rewarding inept proposals. In all honesty, we should be concerned about this possibility in the Japanese-style system.

The Western-style suggestion system is stricter. Since most of the proposals will be rejected as unsuitable after evaluation, employees often feel frustrated by the system. This is why very good ideas sometimes get thrown out, and people often do not bother to come up with suggestions at all. The stage is set for such circumstances.

THE POSITION OF KAIZEN TEIAN IN THE MANAGEMENT SYSTEM

What position does improvement proposal activity occupy in the overall system of management? Since this activity is a companywide activity, it necessarily involves a link between the activity and management. A proposal system should become an integral part of the management system, and it should also be included in the management strategy of a company.

Increasing Profit through Continuous Improvement

The minimum condition defining the objective of most corporate activity is to create profit. A business can exist over time only if it can turn a profit; only then does its continued existence make sense. Added value is the difference between the sales volume of a product and its cost. Most corporate activity, then, tends toward two basic objectives. It is necessary to do one of the following:

- increase sales
- keep costs down

Various strategies and tactics can be used to achieve these two objectives, but most of them can be broadly classified as major innovations or kaizen (continuous improvement).

Two trends and two methods for creating added value

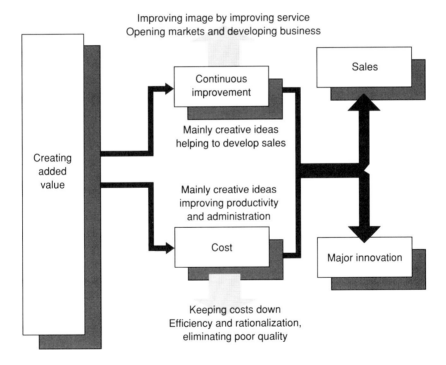

Major innovations bring about dramatic progress, but they require advanced technology and investments. On the other hand, small but cumulative improvements can be made by everyone on a daily basis according to his or her abilities. These improvements bring results that are modest, but numerous and frequent.

Major innovations tend to be an appropriate strategy for responding to market conditions in high-growth periods when the market is gradually expanding. The kaizen approach is very labor-intensive and seems a much more cumbersome and sluggish method to use in such periods.

Under the innovation approach, employees are strongly encouraged to become top-class innovators, while they are, of course, expected to work diligently. But less important suggestions from employees who simply want to change this or that are not particularly welcome in the rush to grand inventions, since they tend to slow things down.

Unlike the strategy of a responsive approach to each proposal, the major innovation strategy is very effective when the objective is to establish market dominance, push out competing companies, and gradually acquire a majority share. Substantial capital investments and expensive development of new products, expansion of production facilities, and expansion of the sales network all require a strong and resolute leadership; companies that are too slow will not survive.

But is this approach also appropriate for a mature, diversified market? A single major innovation will probably not win such a market once and for all. It is not possible to keep fine-tuning product specifications and standards in response to gradually changing market needs unless major innovations are also accompanied by a continuous improvement strategy.

The ideas and resourcefulness of people who work directly on the front lines of sales and production, and the communication of these ideas, are indispensable for this fine-tuning. Moreover, continuous improvement ideas do not require extensive investments of the type required for major innovations.

Kaizen is something that anyone can join in, every day, as long as it feels good to do so.

This is why kaizen, or continuous improvement, has become one of the most important tools of managerial strategy, as it creates a system that channels information and experience from every company employee. This type of proposal activity is known as an implemented improvement proposal system.

Systems that use complaint boxes or that simply collect suggestions differ significantly from systems that strive for implemented improvement proposals. These older systems are unrelated to managerial strategy; they were designed as a supplement to other mechanisms, an extra effort that managers should not count on. Regulations for such systems usually send the message that "You may make a suggestion." This can be interpreted to mean that it is all right if you make a proposal, but it is also all right if you do not.

The attitude behind an implemented improvement proposal system, on the other hand, is that employees are innovative and therefore are expected to have proposals. It is no longer "all right" to decline to make small improvements, for a simple reason — they have become an indispensable tool of the management strategy.

TWO DIRECTIONS IN KAIZEN TEIAN ACTIVITY

Kaizen improvement proposals are analyzed in the figure on page 26. Since the objective of corporate activity is to create profit, the objective of continuous improvement proposal activities is to increase profit as well.

Just as there are two methods that can be used to increase profit, so are there two basic directions in kaizen teian activity:

- ideas for increasing sales
- ideas for keeping costs down

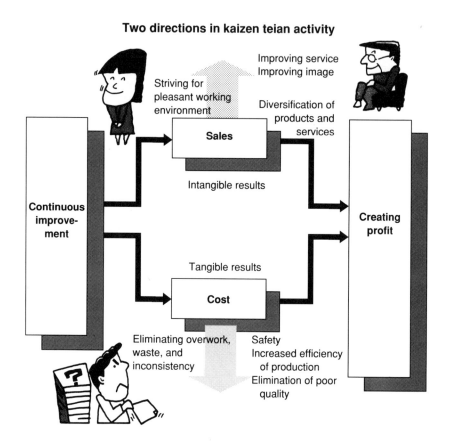

Two directions in kaizen teian activity

Proposals to Keep Costs Down

You keep costs down by working more efficiently; by eliminating low quality, overwork, waste, and inconsistency; and by constantly bringing forward creative proposals that help reduce costs as much as possible.

Most of the kaizen teian improvements designed to improve production at the workplace fall into this category. More often than not, these innovations result from things that workers notice in their workplace, so the effect of such improvement can usually be measured easily.

It is more difficult to measure intangible factors such as the boost to worker morale that results from creative improvements in the workplace or place of production. Yet these factors too are linked indirectly to keeping costs down, as they help to increase productivity. Nevertheless, when we speak of kaizen, we generally mean improvements that have the immediate effect of helping to reduce costs. This aspect of continuous improvement is usually valued highly.

Proposals to Increase Sales

Continuous improvement proposals linked to increased sales include ideas for improving service, product image, product selection, display methods, quality of goods, and similar innovations. These improvement ideas arise most commonly in the areas of marketing, sales, and service. As a company matures, proposals of this type gain importance. On the other hand, it is virtually impossible to measure the direct effect of such innovations on improved sales, because sales results are influenced by many complex factors.

Quality control and improvement proposal activity originated in production departments, and for a long time many argued that such activities could never be applied to sales or service departments. The concept of kaizen in these sectors is indeed very different; one cannot simply borrow systems and rules from the production sector and apply them directly to other areas. Today we are studying management methods and systems that have been applied in various types of business at various stages of development, and devising new methods and systems. Many service departments, beginning with finance, distribution, and sales, have developed their own distinct kaizen movements focusing on improved information processing.

The difference between kaizen in manufacturing and kaizen in service and sales is one of emphasis. The manufacturing sector emphasizes simplification and elimination of waste, whereas the service sector focuses on variety, fashion, popularity, atmosphere, image, and attractive appearance. In fact, improvements aimed at rationalization of products and elimination of waste are sometimes counterproductive in nonmanufacturing departments and companies.

The situation is complicated by the fact that improvements in nonmanufacturing sectors are not designed for material things such as products and machines. They are primarily aimed at that most erratic and troublesome of creatures, the human being. That is why the kaizen methods and the training for those methods must be different. It is not surprising that, when the know-how that was first developed in the manufacturing industry was transposed to service and sales sectors, the initial period was very confusing. Only now are we beginning to make some sense of this confusion.

THREE AIMS AND THREE STAGES

The kaizen movement has the following three objectives:

1. *Participation* — development and activation of the organizational structure
2. *Development of skills* — improvement of performance on the job
3. *Effects* — classified as tangible and intangible

Building Employee Participation in Work and in Planning

The most important aim of the kaizen movement is employee participation. No matter what their attitude and where they work, employees can solve their problems and generate creative proposals only if they feel that this role is vital for their job.

**Comparison of the Objectives of Proposal Systems
in Japan and the United States**

Objective	Importance attributed		Description
	Japan	United States	
1. Conscious participation in company management (voluntary bottom-up activity)	Great	Medium	1. Increases the sense of belonging in a company 2. Improves cooperation as well as communication within the company 3. Improves motivation and active participation in work
2. Training and skills development (bottom-up activity as it relates to skills)	Medium	Small	1. Raises employee awareness of their work and encourages innovation on a regular basis 2. Improves problem-solving and kaizen ability 3. Speeds up on-the-job training through proposals
3. Effect (profit-oriented bottom-up activity)	Small	Great	1. Tangible results: improves efficiency of operations, reduces prime costs, eliminates poor quality 2. Intangible results: improves safety, quality, environment, and service

Note: This comparison is general, since there are non-Japanese companies in the United States that use the Japanese style, and Japanese companies that have adopted the American system of proposals.

Kaizen is in fact nothing more than displaying the common sense and skills that are required in order to do a job properly. Anyone can keep on improving his or her work. Since this is something everyone can do, it is possible to require all employees to participate.

Continuous improvement brings about progress in small but frequent steps. Selective participation of employees is not sufficient to this effort. Profit is ultimately created only if all employees work together, wherever they may be working.

Why is there so much emphasis on total employee participation? The reason is that a "bottom-up" movement like kaizen teian is based on trust in the natural aspirations and skills of each individual.

Douglas McGregor's Theory Y offers six points that reinforce the conviction that every employee has the ability to do kaizen:

1. It is natural for human beings to bring the same effort to work as they do to play. This effort is voluntary and spontaneous.
2. Human beings can control their own conduct once they agree on a certain objective.
3. Human beings strive for self-actualization and fulfillment of their potential.
4. People are usually ready to assume responsibility when conditions allow them to do so.
5. It is not true that only some people are endowed with creativity. Everyone possesses the capacity to be creative and inventive.
6. Modern corporations do not make the best use of the intellectual capabilities of their employees.*

Corporations that have introduced a kaizen teian system, whether they are conscious of it or not, must presume that all of their employees have latent abilities, and they must expect them to put this hidden potential to work. If they did not believe in this hidden potential, they would probably not bother with continuous improvement activities.

---

* See Douglas McGregor, *The Human Side of Enterprise* (New York: McGraw-Hill, 1960).

Developing the Skills of Employees

The second objective of the kaizen movement is to support the development of employees' skills. This objective should be approached from two very important perspectives. First, companies need to cultivate the active skills of employees. These are what enable people to surpass the status quo by making improvements. The kaizen teian movement makes it possible to point out and devise creative improvements without fear of reprimand by supervisors, something that was rarely possible in the past. In other words, kaizen teian makes it possible for the pupils to do better than the teachers. Whereas previous training stressed the need to meet established standard levels of performance, continuous improvement breaks up this standard, taking advantage of a boundless potential that can be developed to create improved standards.

In a test at school, the best companies could earn no higher score than 100 percent. In the real world, however, there is no upper limit for continuous improvements, so a company could conceivably achieve 120 or even 200 percent. The ceiling is determined mainly by the enterprising spirit of employees, and by their determination to achieve their objectives and to solve problems. Creative ability, then, is not something bestowed on a select few; rather, it is present in everyone, needing only to be developed through a person's initiative. Where there is a will, there is a way.

Second, companies need to create channels of communication between supervisors and those working under them. Although workers submit the proposals, it is the supervisors who must prepare a mechanism that makes this activity possible, and they must also set this mechanism in motion.

It is inevitable that some worker proposals will conflict in one way or another with what the supervisor had in mind. When a proposal is unacceptable from a more seasoned point of view, the supervisor faces a dilemma. He or she might respond by saying, "Creative thinking is healthy, but on the other hand . . . ," or, "I understand what you mean, but . . . ." The employee who had the idea may have been expecting to receive an excellent evaluation and to see his or her proposed measures adopted on the spot.

The supervisor's job is to coach the workers and advise them of things to consider to improve their proposals.

This type of conflict is not a bad thing. On the contrary, it represents a perfect opportunity for on-the-job employee training (OJT). The exchange of opinions involved strengthens the link between workers and their supervisors. Proposal activity can be seen as a real test of the capabilities and tolerance of supervisors.

Supervisors who grumble that "we get only lousy proposals because we have nothing but morons working in our company," have an attitude that employees are bound to find offensive. Such a stance is often caused by the limited abilities and talents of the supervisors themselves. If it prevails, the proposal activity will dry up.

One condition of employee skills development is a continuous flow of proposals. If the proposals are few and far between, they will be ineffective as opportunities for on-the-job training. Like athletes who must train daily and persistently, employees develop their creative improvement capacity by practicing it all the time on their job. Only then will the results follow.

Focusing on Effect through Continuous Improvement

The third objective of kaizen activities is effect — the proposal should bring some effective results. Ultimately, increasing profit is a requirement for every form of corporate activity. However, there are no shortcuts to good results; participation and development of skills must come first. These two elements are fundamental to the kaizen teian movement.

Accordingly, this movement takes a form different from that of proposal movements in the West, which tend to stress "buying innovations" or "ideas for cash." Under the Japanese-style system, even proposals judged to have little effect receive a token monetary "participation" award. This creates a climate conducive to proposal activity and to good morale.

Creating a Kaizen Teian Policy that Corresponds to Stages of Activity

The three objectives just discussed correspond to the three stages of development in kaizen teian activity:

Stage 1: In which employees are encouraged simply to participate in the activity

Stage 2: In which employees can develop their abilities to make creative proposals

Stage 3: In which the effect of the proposals is emphasized

We recommend that companies thinking of introducing a kaizen teian system do so in these three stages. There are many examples of companies that ignored this gradual development, and saw their efforts fail. Although it is certainly possible to chance upon a very effective proposal even in the initial stage, the danger is that managers and supervisors will get carried away by this success and expect the same results next time. Then they are apt to be disappointed. After all, novice players are not very firm on their feet; even if they win one play, chances are that they will lose the next one, and probably the game as well.

Smart managers, on the other hand, do not assume that all employees will hit a home run right away. Someone learning baseball must first get used to the ball, then learn how to hit and how to reach first base; only after he or she has learned all these steps is the training complete.

Managing proposal activity is not so different. Good managers will not be dazzled by an accidental success. Rather, they promote proposal activity with the levels of achievement of all the employees in mind. If making innovative proposals does not become second nature to most employees, then the hurdle is set too high and people will stumble.

The most important indicators of progress are, in stage 1, the number of proposals and the percentage of employees who take part in the activity; in stage 2, the percentage of proposals that can be adopted and how many of them are in fact implemented; and in stage 3, the efficiency and economic effect of proposals. Once a company meets the requirements of one stage, it should move forward with the next objectives in sight. Admittedly, this is not easy, since as we said before, the ultimate objective is always "better efficiency."

A MECHANISM AND A STRATEGY

The essential components of proposal activity can be thought of as (1) a *mechanism* and (2) a *strategy* that makes this mechanism work. In contemporary terms, these components can be compared to hardware and software. The mechanism is the passive element, requiring an organizational system, a structure, rules, and so on. It can also be presented through special proposal forms, guidebooks, posters, and other things that will attract attention.

The active component — the thing needed to drive the mechanism — is the strategy. It consists of campaigns, events, and training and education sessions. It also requires actions such as interactive work to encourage worker participation, as well as feedback, advice, counseling, and guidance.

The Link between Mechanism and Strategy

Mechanism
- system
- organization
- regulations
- awards system
- evaluation standards
- proposal forms

Proposal activity

- education and training
- campaigns
- promotional activities
- encouragement
- guidance and assistance

Strategy

Simple Things Work Best

Somewhere in this world there is probably a company that has established its very own proposal system with perfect regulations prepared by legal specialists so as to cover all the bases and possibilities. Such regulations would be beautifully printed and bound, and they would be carefully stored in a locked display cabinet along with other valuables. Although the people at such a company may profess faith in proposal activity, it is doubtful that they have ever actually engaged in any. On the contrary, this kind of reverence would be typical of a company whose employees were oblivious to the purpose of a proposal system.

There are also companies where the opposite is true. Proposal regulations in such companies might consist of no more than a few rules handwritten on plain paper. For some reason, it is in just such companies that excellent innovations will come to light. Proposals will be submitted frequently, even though supervisors complain that the regulations and system of bonus payments keep changing.

This paradox reveals much about the relationship between mechanism and strategy. The mechanism can be quite simple; in fact, it can be just a rough plan. The details can be ironed out when the real activity is in progress. Sometimes the workplace managers can be put in charge of the final details.

By contrast, putting in place strict evaluation standards and regulations, as if trying to lay down the law, may be futile. Even the smallest innovation destroys existing conditions, since it represents a creative movement, establishing methods and ideas previously unknown. These methods and ideas often have no precedent. Even if detailed regulations and standards are created, creative ideas will often exceed their range.

Development Requires Suitable Conditions for Each Stage

It is important to establish a link between the mechanism and the strategy. Nothing is more doomed to failure than a mechanism that does not fit the strategy.

To give an example, if the goal of the first stage is to secure full participation of employees in proposal activity and to make such activity second nature to employees, then it makes little sense to use standardized proposal forms that must be filled in as prescribed. It is more appropriate to use simple memo forms that would be fun to write.

As the strategy changes in stage 2, so should the mechanisms. Rather than using blank forms that encourage people to write down ideas just as they occur, companies should use proposal forms with columns, so that workers can describe the present situation, list the causes of problems, and outline the proposed countermeasures. This type of form will reinforce analytical thinking and articulate clearly the methods and steps of the process of creative improvement.

The same is true of the other mechanisms — rules, evaluation standards, and the awards system. All must change as the strategy changes.

Like a living organism, proposal activity constantly changes and grows. That is why it is necessary to continually adjust and modify the mechanism as well as the strategy. It would be silly to keep a growing child in last year's clothes.

THREE ESSENTIAL FACTORS FOR SUCCESSFUL BOTTOM-UP ACTIVITY

A bottom-up activity such as a kaizen teian program must be managed on a continuous basis. If it is to bring positive results, it must have the following three characteristics:

- It must be a compelling force.
- It must create motivation and incentives.
- It must be educational and must be instrumental in developing skills.

You need to develop these three vital elements in appropriate steps, keeping the right balance between their functions.

Three essential factors of bottom-up activity

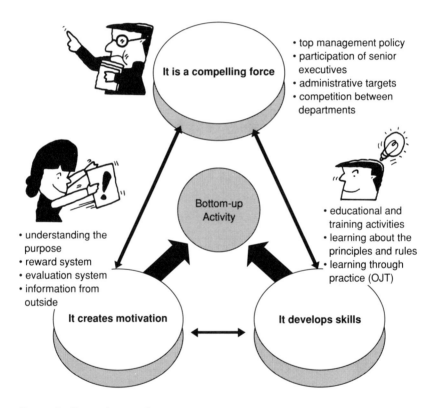

It is a compelling force

- top management policy
- participation of senior executives
- administrative targets
- competition between departments

Bottom-up Activity

- educational and training activities
- learning about the principles and rules
- learning through practice (OJT)

- understanding the purpose
- reward system
- evaluation system
- information from outside

It creates motivation

It develops skills

Step 1: Creating a Compelling Force

The ultimate compelling force is the attitude of the company's top managers. A corporate activity cannot survive without guidance and support from top management.

Superficially, bottom-up activity may appear to be an independent activity, but interpreting it as such would be a great mistake. The law of inertia applies to the real world, and breaking up this force requires another force.

Another compelling factor is associated with the administrative structure. Many bottom-up activities movements have failed because the formation of an administrative structure was ignored or misunderstood, and the activity never had a chance to develop properly. In the final analysis, the managers are in charge of the various departments, and they should be responsible as well for any activity that improves the management of business.

The word *independence* can be easily misinterpreted as meaning that there is no need for an administrative structure. But such an interpretation would not result in a successful movement. Since one of the main aspects of a kaizen teian program is its appeal to every employee of the company, it must be supported by a well-functioning organizational structure.

Promotion of a bottom-up activity like an improvement proposal system is an important duty of every manager, starting with the CEO. Depending on conditions, it may be also necessary to develop management targets, promote interdepartmental competition, and find other ways to enhance the "compelling force" and develop the strategy of the system.

Step 2: Creating Motivation and Incentives

Although creating a compelling top-down appeal is the fastest and most immediately effective way to promote improvement activity, a genuine kaizen movement requires more than that. Mistakes can be costly, because each mistake takes away from employee spontaneity. If managers exert force on employees, using quotas and other means for leverage, they will achieve an effect opposite to the one intended.

While the compelling force is useful in the initial stages before the improvement proposal movement picks up speed, there is always a need to educate employees so that they understand why they are doing the activities and what their objectives are. Otherwise, the employees will not remain motivated and eager to work. Above all, they should understand clearly what their company is gaining from their participation. If the intention is to create a system that looks good to company managers, few will take it seriously.

The development of a genuine bottom-up activity depends on two things — how management will profit from this activity, and how employees will benefit from it. It boils down to this: the official policy of the company must be reflected in the real intentions of the management.

Step 3: Educating Employees and Developing Skills

You have completed the initial stage, creating a compelling force, and you have also come through the second stage, having motivated employees. But that does not necessarily mean that from now on the movement will progress without a hitch. There is a third component: cultivating the skills of the employees.

A movement based only on willingness to participate has obvious limitations. With participation as the only criterion, it would be easy to give high marks to superficial and temporary measures that are not improvements in the real sense of the word. To bring about concrete and substantial results, employees must also acquire and develop improvement techniques, skills, thinking patterns, and other important abilities.

A new level of development becomes necessary, one discarding impulsive and sporadic activity for a more systematic and scientific approach. This is not to say that all employees should go through a highly specialized educational process. All that is needed is an explanation of the basic concepts behind a given job. The important thing is to reinforce workers' understanding of the reasons they do the things they do — things they take for granted.

A Graphic Illustration of a Kaizen Teian System

The chart on pages 42-43 illustrates the workings of the kaizen teian system. Studying the chart will help you to understand the role of management in this system, as well as the direction and objectives of improvement proposal activity.

At this point it is probably clear that the kaizen teian system and the Western-style suggestion box system are two different things. The kaizen teian system can be described as a vehicle through which creative direction is injected into an organization and through which the boundless potential hidden in every employee is unleashed.

Whether this magnificent system can be used to full advantage depends on how it is positioned in management. Kaizen teian improvements are at least as important as major reforms and innovations. Innovations that are not accompanied by kaizen will never be fully implemented and their effect will be limited; continuous improvements, on the other hand, are effective whether or not they're accompanied by major innovations. Thus innovation and kaizen are two wheels of one cart that carries both the corporate system and management's goals for the company.

DISCUSSION QUESTIONS

What does *teian* mean?

Name three differences between the kaizen teian system and the Western-style suggestion box system.

What are the three objectives of the kaizen movement?

The Role of Kaizen Teian in the Corporate Management System

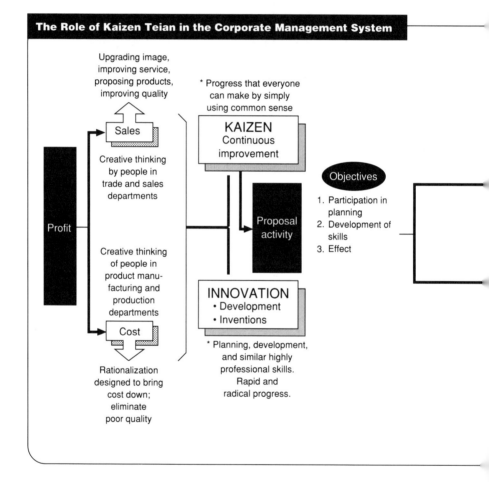

Upgrading image,
improving service,
proposing products,
improving quality

* Progress that everyone
  can make by simply
  using common sense

Sales

Creative thinking
by people in
trade and sales
departments

KAIZEN
Continuous
improvement

Objectives

Profit

Proposal
activity

1. Participation in
   planning
2. Development of
   skills
3. Effect

Creative thinking
of people in
product manu-
facturing and
production
departments

INNOVATION
• Development
• Inventions

Cost

Rationalization
designed to bring
cost down;
eliminate
poor quality

* Planning, development,
  and similar highly
  professional skills.
  Rapid and
  radical progress.

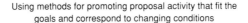

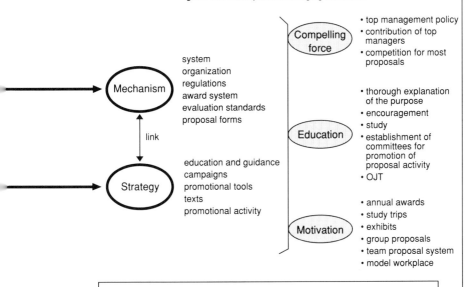

Using methods for promoting proposal activity that fit the
goals and correspond to changing conditions

Mechanism

system
organization
regulations
award system
evaluation standards
proposal forms

link

Strategy

education and guidance
campaigns
promotional tools
texts
promotional activity

Compelling force

• top management policy
• contribution of top managers
• competition for most proposals

Education

• thorough explanation of the purpose
• encouragement
• study
• establishment of committees for promotion of proposal activity
• OJT

Motivation

• annual awards
• study trips
• exhibits
• group proposals
• team proposal system
• model workplace

Initial "urging" can make improvements attractive; thus it speeds up the process
and makes it more efficient. On the other hand, in order to achieve qualitative
improvements and to create a new, substantially different consciousness, it is
necessary to keep educating employees and to motivate them by constant
promotional activities.

PART TWO

Walking Suggestion Boxes

The traditional suggestion box, which hangs passively on the wall, awaiting written suggestions, is obsolete. Companies today need "walking suggestion boxes" — managers and supervisors who collect good ideas from every employee of the company. Part two of this book treats the concepts behind this philosophy.

3

Creating a System of
Walking Suggestion Boxes

THE SUGGESTION BOX IS OBSOLETE

The term *suggestion box* calls forth an image of a manager fishing for a few ideas, using a bonus award as bait.

This image is the relic of a bygone era. Today few success-ful maintain this type of system for gathering employee ideas. Most have replaced their old "suggestion box" systems with systems that invite proposals for simple improvements that can be implemented by employees themselves.

Rarely are there suggestion boxes in workplaces that have active systems for continuous improvement proposal activities. Moreover, in those companies that do use suggestion boxes as their "system," the boxes serve as little more than wall decora-tion and the proposal activity itself is lackluster.

Obviously, the difference between the two systems does not lie in the presence or absence of a suggestion box in the workplace; rather, it lies in the attitude of employees and man-agers toward improvement proposal activity. Companies that have intense proposal activity may use proposal boxes as deco-rative symbols of the activity, but the activity's success never rests on the presence of those boxes.

A traditional suggestion box system differs from a continu-ous improvement proposal system in both purpose and concept; there are substantial differences between the two systems in terms of management, promotion methods, evaluation stan-dards, and other variables.

The continuous improvement proposal system involves a new school of thought among managers and supervisors. It demands a new attitude, expressed in questions such as "how can I encourage people to come forward with more proposals?" or "what can I do to create a more dynamic proposal activity?" The conventional system of promoting people who have clever ideas is not always the best way to inspire loyalty to the company. Before long the proposal box will be covered by a layer of dust, and in the end the business may suffer and decline.

When that happens, people may complain that "systems like that work fine at Toyota or Matsushita, but things are differ-ent at *our* company," or "it's okay to do this in a manufacturing company, but not in *our* line of business," and so on. But do these statements have any basis?

THE ERA OF WALKING SUGGESTION BOXES

What is the nature of this continuous improvement proposal system? It is a dynamic system of "walking suggestion boxes" — a new system in which immediate supervisors, the proposal system promotion staff, and others come to each employee in person. They work with their subordinates and colleagues, hear their complaints, and learn directly from them about new ideas and innovative proposals.

Walking Suggestion Boxes

A traditional suggestion box system usually sends these messages to employees:

1. Employees can come forward with proposals.
2. It is all right if employees make proposals.
3. It is all right if employees don't make proposals.

In other words, under a suggestion box system, it does not matter whether people come forward with a proposal or not. Usually this means that the management does not provide additional ingredients such as financial rewards and similar incentives.

If managers tell people to "come forward with a proposal if you have a good idea," they are also telling them that unless they have a good idea they do not need to bother bringing up any proposals. The idea is that the suggestion box will "swallow" only good proposals.

A Passive Suggestion Box

Under such a system it is impossible for people to voice a constructive and meaningful opinion. No matter how you look at it, it is a lazy system.

Can such a passive system really be effective for gathering ideas and innovative proposals in this day and age? Is this way of doing things really going to strengthen a company and improve its competitiveness? The answer is most likely no.

This is where a walking suggestion box system is different. Sometimes it is necessary to be aggressive in getting proposals. Some managers even write up proposals on behalf of their employees.

Unless managers and supervisors take such an approach, people will not come forward with innovative proposals that are really worth something. Conversely, if they embrace the new approach, they can get innovative ideas from employees in every workplace, ideas that will help to solve problems and improve the way people work.

Today corporations can no longer afford not to care whether people generate ideas for solving workplace problems. Therefore, managers must proactively solicit ideas from every employee to draw out ideas that will pay off.

There is no other choice.

INTRODUCING AND DEVELOPING A SUITABLE SYSTEM

There are big differences in the significance attributed to proposal systems by various companies. Some companies pay minimum awards of ¥5,000 (around $35) per proposal, while others pay only ¥50 (less than one dollar). Some companies request epochal ideas that will significantly improve business results, while other companies expect a series of small personal and innovative ideas.

Companies that put up fancy suggestion boxes, complete with lock and key, often receive few good suggestions. In many such companies, the suggestion system becomes a burden; few innovations will be implemented, as managers and reviewers are too busy evaluating and processing the suggestions.

Some companies form evaluation committees consisting of people in key positions. The managers who are responsible for specific areas decide whether to accept a proposal and determine the amount of the award.

Although idea proposal systems vary in the route through which proposals are submitted, the manner in which they are accepted, the method by which they are evaluated, the bonus offered, and so on, the main distinction lies in what is *required* from a proposal and what is the *purpose* of a proposal.

For example, idea proposal systems can be classified according to the types of ideas the company is looking for:

- proposals for office work improvements
- simple "ideas"
- direct petitions to upper management
- general suggestion competitions (no special criteria)
- proposals for new product development
- proposals for developing new business

Each company has a different method for developing its type of proposal activity.

There are also companies that say "just give us a proposal — it can be anything at all." When proposals are received, they are processed and evaluated, then put to practical use. At other companies the system does not allow for thorough evaluation of proposals, so confusion results and workers lose confidence in management.

Whatever the purpose of a system, success depends on whether the means to achieve that purpose is suitable for the purpose. When some companies say that they have a "system" but get no results, it is often because the purpose of the proposal system does not correspond with the system that is used. In the worst cases, the managers and employees are not sure from the start about the reason for introducing a certain system and the purpose of that system.

Some companies simply imitate other companies' systems. But such imitation is bound to meet with resistance at some point. When that happens, the sham will be exposed and only the form will remain.

Only a few outstanding companies persevere to develop a proposal system in which the purpose is clear to everyone. They keep improving the system and striving to develop methods that best suit this purpose. Often, they abandon passive suggestion boxes on the wall and turn instead to walking suggestion boxes.

Improving Office Work — In the Office

Most companies that want to improve administrative work and the way the workplace and jobs are organized have switched to a system that uses managers as walking suggestion boxes. The reason for this switch is the need to solve problems that are encountered on every job and in every workplace. These problems can be solved only if supervisors and their employees pool their knowledge right where they work to find viable solutions.

The ideas submitted through an impersonal suggestion box system are often evaluated far away from the place where the problem arose. It makes far more sense to solve the problem on the spot where it occurs.

DIRECT PETITIONS TO TOP MANAGEMENT: A REMNANT OF THE FEUDAL SYSTEM

One of the most firmly entrenched concepts of suggestion systems in Japan is the idea of making direct petitions to the people at the top, bypassing those in the middle.

This type of direct petition system (*meyasubako*) was introduced in 1721 by Yoshimune Tokugawa, the eighth shogun of the Tokugawa dynasty. The purpose of this box was to get a sampling of opinions of the common people, who had good reason to complain about their treatment under the local lords. The word went out: "Share your thoughts with us. If we find them useful, we will reward you in appreciation of your services." This was a formidable idea in an era when decapitation was a common punishment for people who stepped outside their social rank. In reality, however, whatever suggestions were received were used only if they suited the selfish interests of the feudal government. Warm appreciation was expressed only if the officials deemed it appropriate.

Nevertheless, the notion of a box for direct petitions to the top is still firmly rooted in some modern corporations. Just as the *meyasubako* boxes existed to inform the shogun of the oppression of the peasants by their evil feudal lords, the suggestion box today is still seen as a tool for use against mid-level company managers, who presumably cannot be trusted, so that the voice of the people (lower-level employees) can be heard over their heads.

A Direct Petition System

This is certainly one way for ideas and reports, and sometimes also grievances and demands, from lower-ranked employees to reach the upper levels of management. But is such a system really effective? Maybe it has some value if the organizational structure has become irrelevant, in which case it will release some steam. Also, this type of system can be useful after a change of management, to inform the new executive about employee opinions. To continue maintaining and using such a system, however, makes no sense. A direct petition system does not make good use of an organization's functions. There is something wrong with a system in which employees must appeal directly to upper management to be heard. Fundamental problems exist in the company, irrespective of the proposal system it may have; it is absurd to think that such problems can be solved through a direct petition system.

If the management in fact used such a system, what would be the results? Top management would receive hundreds, perhaps thousands, of requests, grievances, and suggestions from the employees. To handle the onslaught, top managers would use only ideas that are "convenient" for their purposes. The system was designed to get around the self-interest of those in the middle, but it is, after all, a system from the feudal age. If top managers hear what employees have to say but act on only those ideas convenient for them to use, then they are only pretending to be democratic. In the end, such a system is counterproductive, eroding organizational structures rather than invigorating them.

A more vitalized organization can be achieved if people are allowed to identify and solve their own problems. A proposal system in which proposals are evaluated far from their source does not make for a resilient organizational structure.

The feudal era was abolished more than a thousand years ago. The elements of an imperial system do not belong in the organizational structures of modern companies.

BEYOND THE GENERAL SUGGESTION COMPETITION

The same principle that gave rise to suggestion boxes lies behind suggestion competitions. Companies have contests to choose the best employee idea for naming a new product, to gather ideas for new lines of business, and so on. These competitions can be elaborate affairs, advertised throughout the company to elicit as many suggestions from as many employees as possible.

It is popular today to hold contests in which "amateurs" contribute their ideas and other things, and sometimes interesting ideas are indeed discovered in this way. This type of contest provides relief from the daily work routine; it allows employees to express their creative ideas, builds a sense of belonging to the company, and can be a lot of fun. But expecting such contests to have a significant impact on the future of the company or to solve burning issues is a sign of serious trouble in the company.

DISCUSSION QUESTIONS

What is meant by the term "walking suggestion box"?

How does it differ from the suggestion box system?

4

From Company-oriented Suggestions to Job-oriented Proposals

THE PITFALLS OF MAKING PROPOSALS FOR OTHERS TO IMPLEMENT

One obstacle to the development of proposal activity is the notion that improvement proposals should relate to the company in general or to other departments. Some companies even have special regulations clearly stating that ideas relating to an employee's own job will not be acknowledged as proposals, seemingly making it impossible for employees to try to improve their jobs.

Although many companies follow this line, it is the wrong approach if the aim is an active proposal movement. Ninety-nine percent of such companies suffer setbacks in their proposal activity because of this "company-oriented idea" approach, and their results are not very good. Unless this obstacle is removed, a proposal system will not work, no matter what other means — big contests, inspirational speakers, and the like — management may use.

Some companies that used this restricted system have changed their policy to emphasize making proposals that relate

Getting Stuck Trying to Change the Company or Other Departments

A Japanese fable describes a foolish monkey that grasps and holds on to a large object in a jar, then thinks it is stuck when it can't pull out its hand. Managers and suggestions promoters who hold tight to the notion of "company-related" suggestions find themselves in a similar bind.

to improvements in the proposer's own job. With this new interpretation, a silly notion is cleared away. Today such companies represent the foremost trend in the improvement proposal movement, with proposal activity that focuses on improvements that the proposal maker can implement. This is the *kaizen teian* system (continuous improvement through implemented proposals).

This proposal system of implementable improvements has the following characteristics:

1. Proposals should relate to the proposer's own workplace and job.
2. Since the purpose is to improve jobs rather than to generate abstract ideas, these proposals should be innovations that can be implemented.
3. These improvements should be effective, but — even more important — they should be seen as a way to energize people on the job and to develop their creative capabilities.

The logic behind a system of improvements that can be implemented at the workplace seems obvious. But "obvious" truths are often obscured. Ironically, many companies that profess a need for new ideas are themselves unable to change their attitudes about creative ideas.

THE TREND TOWARD IMPLEMENTED IMPROVEMENTS

Proposal systems in many companies have undergone revisions of the type shown in the following V-shaped graph. When the system is first introduced, there are many proposals, perhaps because it is a novelty. The system works smoothly for about three years, after which it develops problems. Fewer and fewer proposals come in, until finally, at about year 5, none come in at all.

Many companies that reach this point either eliminate proposal activity or settle for a period of dormancy. However, some companies resume activities after only a brief suspension. The hibernation is followed by a significantly increased effort, so that these companies are at present slightly above average for their

Revision of the Proposal System

industries when it comes to the number and value of improvement proposals. What is happening at these companies?

Conventional logic would suggest that they did one of the following things:

- drastically increased the amount of awards for proposals
- relaxed the requirements for submitting proposals
- put a lot of effort into campaigns and promotional events, education, and training

All of these guesses would be wrong; in fact, the reverse is true. The changes they ultimately made were

- lowering the minimum award from ¥500 to only ¥200 (a change of approximately $3.30 to $1.30 at ¥150/$1)
- tightening the requirements for submitting proposals by limiting the content to innovations relating to the proposer's job

Substantial change is never achieved simply by a quick shot in the arm and improvised half-measures. This will be clear to anyone who observes how things develop after an apparent success. Measures that are merely clever tricks are not conducive to positive development and hence can never lead to permanent growth.

The changes adopted by the companies that made comebacks after a decline in proposal activity involved switching from a system of abstract company-oriented proposals to a system of implementable job-oriented improvements. Once these companies revised their systems, proposal activity picked up speed and energy. The companies that now have successful continuous improvement proposal activities all experienced a similar transition.

The Fun Is Gone

Let's consider why problems begin to appear after three years of company-oriented suggestion activities. At first, people are taken with the idea that they can suggest anything — as long as it relates to the company in general — and suggestions for other departments flood in from all directions. Most of these suggestions would be more accurately characterized as complaints and demands.

During the first year or so, these ideas and demands somehow get adopted. People often remember these proposals well and are full of praise for the measures that were implemented. In time, however, suggestions start piling up on the desks of the review committee and decisions are deferred. People who inquire are told that "we're working on it," or "we are looking into it." This is a good indication that the management is running out of elbow room. The initial suggestion fever has vanished and the atmosphere is turning sour. Soon the number of suggestions falls dramatically, until in the end no one bothers to come up with any suggestions at all.

SUGGESTIONS TO OTHER DEPARTMENTS LEAD NOWHERE

The idea behind systems based on suggestions to other departments is to solicit information, ideas, and opinions on every department from disinterested employees. It is an appealing notion: If you are not really responsible for the outcome, then it is easy to tell other departments what to do and how they should do it. A large number of popular proposals can be pulled out of thin air.

The only problem is that the proposals will not be very useful. Workers outside the department cannot understand the effect their proposal will have on people actually experiencing the problem. This fact will not be lost on those inside the department, who are probably doing their work as well as possible and cannot be expected to accept senseless suggestions and demands graciously. They will resent being treated as pawns by people who know nothing about what they do.

With so few of the proposals being adopted, people will lose interest in the system and stop submitting proposals. Then the system will exist in name only.

Of course, some of the ideas submitted are indeed very good. Some people are very perceptive and can point out things that the people in charge would never notice. Occasionally, such suggestions will be welcomed gratefully. But that rarely happens.

More often, proposals submitted from outside the department are unwelcome because they make supervisors look bad, while the person who comes forward with the proposal looks

Proposals from Other Departments

good. The tension between these two positions is bound to prove counterproductive and to lead to organizational problems. Trying to deal with this tension through the proposal system is the wrong approach.

What Happens When Suggestions Are Not Implemented

When a company establishes a proposal system in which the problems of one department are open territory to the people of another department, suggestions are apt to pour in from every quarter. Soon the company is overwhelmed with suggestions, unable to implement even the simplest one. Not just the numbers, but the content of the proposals makes implementation impossible. Some projects would cost a lot of money to carry out. If it is a major proposal, it often involves some risk and a lengthy implementation process. Certainly, the implementation of such projects is much more time-consuming and labor-intensive than the act of making the proposal.

That is why people who are busy trying to do their jobs postpone indefinitely the implementation of suggestions from other departments. If this is the reaction to a proposal that is sincerely meant, surely it is better for employees to concentrate on their own work and stop wasting their time making unappreciated suggestions.

There is nothing wrong with a corporate philosophy that emphasizes receptivity to employee opinions and respect for everyone's viewpoint. In reality, however, a suggestion system based on disinterested viewpoints will always hit a snag under the conditions of real-life problems.

CONTINUOUS IMPROVEMENT IN YOUR OWN WORKPLACE AND JOB

The most effective type of proposal is one that involves continuous improvements in your own workplace and job, especially improvements that you can implement yourself. Such improvements represent a genuine proposal activity.

This is because ideas begin to have a real value only when they are put to work. Ideas that cannot be implemented are meaningless, no matter how dazzling they sound.

The implementation rate for improvements proposed by those closest to the problem is very high. This is because people enjoy carrying out their own ideas and are committed to seeing them work.

Getting the person who raises the idea to implement it is crucial to the proposal's success. All kinds of problems are bound to arise during the implementation process. Constant vigilance and cooperation with others is required. Such a daunting task requires the hand of someone with the knowledge, skills, and interest to ensure a successful outcome. Increasingly, companies are recognizing that the person at the workplace is the best person to solve workplace problems. They have made this concept the cornerstone of a successful proposal system.

The Only True Proposals Are Implemented Ones

Improvement proposal activity is even more advanced in companies where the proposals that are submitted are those that have been already implemented. Such companies often have pre-printed forms for employees to use in reporting implemented work improvements.

At some companies, the policy is to accept *only* implemented proposals. Some would say that a system that collects information about proposals that have already been carried out cannot be called a "proposal" system, and, strictly speaking, they are correct. A number of companies have even changed the name of their systems to "kaizen reporting systems" (their proposal forms are titled "kaizen reports").

However, many companies still use the term *suggestion* out of habit, although they have adopted the new type of implemented proposal system. And other companies use the term *proposal* for any kind of suggestion, implemented or not.

True Proposal Activity Involves a Kaizen Reporting System

The ideal system keeps everyone informed of implemented improvements through a kaizen reporting system. Such a system teaches employees about the kinds of methods that can be used on a certain job, as well as techniques and innovations by way of information contained in circulated forms and reports.

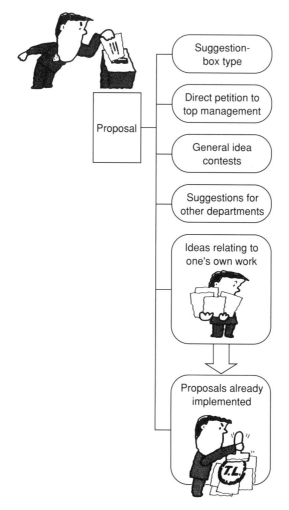

This is a good way to keep everyone informed of the progress of improvement activities. It tends to promote improvements and it is an effective method for speeding up the proposal activity.

To ensure a really efficient system of proposals, it is imperative to let everyone know the real state of affairs and to promote real understanding of the situation, rather than just talking about "improvement activities" all the time. A kaizen reporting system,* which informs everyone about improvements that have been made, is the easiest and ultimately the most effective way to do this. Companies that have embraced this system are finding that it breathes new life into company activities.

DISCUSSION QUESTIONS

What are the advantages and disadvantages of systems that limit proposal activity to suggestions for other departments or for the company as a whole?

What are the defining characteristics of a system of implementable improvements?

What is a kaizen reporting system?

---

* For more about kaizen reporting systems, see *Kaizen Teian 3*, Productivity Press, 1992.

5

Ideas Have Value Only
When Implemented

THE SKILL DEVELOPMENT ASPECT OF
PROPOSAL ACTIVITY

Even today, the term *proposal system* calls forth for many people an image of some traditional suggestion system — passive suggestion boxes, direct petitions to top management, general contests, or suggestions relating to other departments. The main difference between such conventional approaches and modern mainstream systems — proposals for improvements in one's own job or proposals that have been implemented already — is in who is implementing the improvements.

The act of "implementing" something seems to go hand in hand with problems and obstacles. There is a tremendous gap between ideas and their realization. Filling in this void is the true function of proposal activities, and it is precisely in this function where old types of proposal systems are deficient.

From Informing to Implementing

Take a look at the contents of a filled-in suggestion form. What is it describing? First of all, it presents *information*. For example, it notes that "a nail is sticking out on the floor and it is dangerous." A proposal is based on information contained in such a description. When workers overlook something, they will be grateful if someone points it out to them.

The proposal may contain a simple *demand* to "remove the nail." This is one step up from indifference: it calls for someone else to take it out somehow.

An *opinion* goes one step further than a demand. It expresses a fundamental point of view — for example, "You must take that nail out if you want to maintain a safe working environment. And you are responsible for safety at your work-place." The only logical response to an opinion like this is, "OK, you are right."

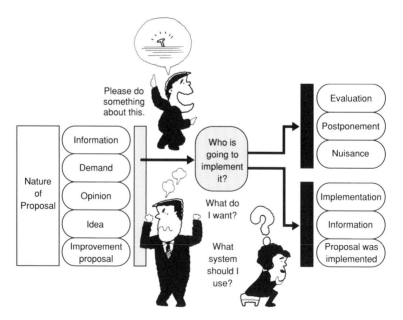

An *idea* goes further still. It assumes that there is a way of dealing with the problem, and is written like this: "Well, how about doing it this way?" From this point on, the value of an idea will keep increasing.

Ideas conceived by people from other departments, who see the situation as outsiders, are sometimes useful. But more often than not, people outside the actual situation pay little attention to cost, safety requirements, and other conditions. This is why in many cases their ideas cannot be implemented.

A *proposal* to take certain measures goes one step further than an idea. Such a proposal selects one idea out of many, according to which one can be implemented. Since it describes in detail how the idea will be realized, the managers in charge can participate in the process by providing their "professional opinions." Once this point is reached, the whole idea becomes much more realistic.

Unfortunately, ideas for other departments stand little chance of getting beyond the initial level. No matter how brilliant an idea is, it makes sense only when it is the basis for a proposal describing which measures should be taken. And this is best done by those who are closest to the problem. Remember that the implementation of an idea is the most important thing.

NO PROGRESS WITHOUT IMPLEMENTATION

When introducing a proposal system, managers in many companies encourage workers to "just come up with some suggestions — anything will do." But this concept of "anything will do" is suspect. Since anything will do, people will gladly come up with *something*. It's fun to order others around, telling them to do this and do that.

In such a system, 99 percent of the submissions will be demands and complaints addressed to other departments. This may make people feel that they are participating in the process, but it will not bear fruit and will eventually lose all momentum.

The reason why so few suggestions are carried out is that most of them receive the response: "We are looking at it." This is merely a face-saving move. The proposal is destined to end up shelved for good. This is how the suggestion system enters stagnancy in many companies.

Implemented Proposals Breathe New Life into the System

But many companies have managed to solve this dilemma. Their method is simple — when the people who make proposals are also made responsible for carrying them out, the percentage of implemented proposals goes up.

Although some people think that implemented proposal systems will produce only a few proposals because it is difficult to carry them out, this is a myth. In fact, the opposite is true. Almost every company that produces a large volume of proposals on a continuous basis recommends a system that uses implemented proposals. This system works because as soon as one idea is implemented, another proposal is made. People are encouraged by their progress and continue to make proposals. The problem with the traditional system, in which the proposal maker was not required to implement the idea, was that suggestions got stuck at the "we're looking into it" stage.

An analysis of "bad proposals" showed that there was often no serious effort to implement the ideas. It is possible that the proposers were pushed by the company to make a suggestion or to just put something in writing. Whatever the reason, the only thing achieved was a suggestion form filled in with something that was a proposal in name only.

These would-be proposals, however, were usually nothing but requests for the company to do this or that, calls for large-scale projects, or no actual suggestion at all. After enough of

Implementating an Idea Is the Best Way to Generate More Ideas

these have come through, even realistic proposals will get a standard polite refusal from the reviewers, a statement that the proposal is too difficult to implement and therefore cannot be used.

Every proposal should be met with a frank response. People making suggestions shouldn't be given the runaround and left wondering whether someone will do something about their idea. This is nothing but a waste of time.

Sometimes there is no intention to carry out suggestions that are submitted. Although people sometimes make proposals without expecting that they will be carried out, the reviewers often think that they must explain all the reasons why such proposals cannot be adopted. They may try to avoid hurting the applicant by saying things like "maybe we can make it work somehow." But too often this is just a pose with no substance to it.

Once the proposal is out in the open, it must be studied to resolve potential problems, complications, needs, and requests. Unless proposals are given proper consideration and closely scrutinized, proposal activity is merely a ruse.

JOB RANGE AND POSSIBILITY OF IMPLEMENTATION

Continually Adding Small Improvements

The focus on workplace improvements and on implemented proposals means that changes introduced will not be major innovations. Because they involve everyday routine work, they will be small projects. But improvement activity lives or dies by small improvements that accumulate over time.

The chart on p. 75 illustrates this point. It shows how a proposal capable of being implemented affects the workplace. The vertical axis shows innovations that relate to an employee's own work and the individual issues that arise in that context; an example is adjusting the height of a chair to a level comfortable for working. This increases work productivity and is good for the person's health besides. Thus, it is an important improvement.

Furthermore, it can be done in a moment. It costs nothing and it does not bother anyone. What's more, there is no need for permission or approval. It can be written up as an implemented improvement right away. The area above the diagonal line on the chart represents improvements that are easily realized and that are very practical. Notice that this area grows smaller as you move to the right on the chart.

The horizontal axis of the chart shows the expanding range of the job, from an employee's own work to other departments in the company and ultimately to the company as a whole. As the area of the bottom triangle indicates, the farther you move

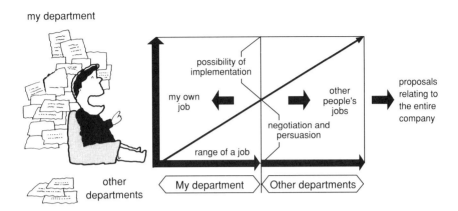

my department

possibility of
implementation

my own
job

other
people's
jobs

proposals
relating to
the entire
company

negotiation and
persuasion

range of a job

other
departments

My department   Other departments

away from your own work, the more complicated it will be to implement an innovation.

Employees proposing improvements must assess how their proposals relate not only to their own work but to that of teammates and of the preceding and following work processes. They must consider whether their proposals involve company-wide factors, such as ideas for increasing the number of customers. When other people are affected and other factors are involved, employees can no longer make solo decisions about improvement ideas. They will have to obtain permission or instructions from a supervisor, or rally the cooperation of other people to make their proposals work.

There is no risk involved in adjusting the height of your own chair to a level that you find comfortable, but you cannot apply the same improvement to other people's chairs. You must consult with those people, get their permission, persuade them, negotiate with them. And they may just tell you to leave them alone.

Gaining Consensus Takes a Special Ability

Not every proposal from an "outsider" is intrusive. There are some good ideas among such proposals. But the further you venture from own job, the more difficult it is to carry out an improvement. That is because you need to convince others of the value of your proposal, a task that requires the art of persuasion.

Proposals involving areas that the proposer is wholly unfamiliar with, such as those from low-level employees dictating management policy, are carried out only rarely. Most employees lack the authority, competence, and capability to implement ideas that affect a wide range of fields outside their own work. On the other hand, proposals involving areas close to the proposer, such as a suggestion for adjusting the height of his or her own chair, are implemented all the time.

Proposals involving the whole company are the ones that reviewers and managers dislike the most. One of the reasons is that it takes a lot of energy and money to implement even a small proposal in every department of the company. Under a well-run proposal system, the response to such a proposal would be: "This is an excellent idea. Why don't you implement it first in your workplace and we will see what happens." This type of pilot implementation will indicate whether the proposal can be implemented on a larger scale.

The narrower the scope of a proposal, the better chance it has of being implemented; this is why it is best to try out an idea first at your own workplace. If it works, you will gain a stronger negotiating position for extending the scope of the improvement to other departments.

KAIZEN LEADS TO THE DEVELOPMENT OF ABILITIES

The principles explained in the chart shown previously are true not just for improvements and proposals but for work relationships in general. The more authority you have, the greater will be your ability to persuade and the larger will be the extent of your influence. Similarly, if you make a proposal, the more experienced you are in the area relevant to the proposal, the better your chances for seeing that proposal realized.

Improvements are usually proposed by people who have mastered the area needing improvement. A good proposal presumes the skills and experience of its author. You are not apt to hear people commenting that "Jane can't do the job well, but she certainly is innovative" — at least not in the context of work-related improvements.

Employees must cultivate their skills and abilities if they want to be able to implement their own ideas. In this respect, improvement activity can also be regarded as development of abilities.

To implement continuous improvement proposals, employees must consult with supervisors and seek their advice, and such communication can be highly instructive. In fact, this is probably the most effective on-the-job training a person can get.

"We're Looking into It" Does Not Promote Employee Development

Old-style suggestion systems offer no such opportunities for employee growth. Ideas are simply dropped in a box, out of the proposers' hands. Proposers have no way of knowing what will happen to the idea — presumably "someone up there" will do something about it. But even if managers do take up the idea, such a system fails to satisfy employees' ambitions to continually improve their jobs on their own.

In companies that have developed implemented proposal systems, proposers never hear responses like "we're looking into it." On the contrary, it is more likely that they will be asked to look more closely at the proposal. This kind of encouragement helps people develop their innovative abilities, which leads to an active proposal movement and builds a company of thoughtful employees.

Proposal activity is useful for purposes other than the development of the employees' creative abilities. It also tests the skills of supervisors and managers. They must be skilled

From "We're Reviewing Your Suggestion" to "Please Look More Closely at Your Proposal"

negotiators to promote the proposals of those working for them and to help make those proposals work in other departments. They must inspire people's trust.

In a way, proposals represent small rebellions and insurrections, and accepting them requires a measure of goodwill on management's part. When goodwill is in short supply — when managers and supervisors are always finding fault with those below — it is impossible to satisfy the self-improvement ambition or to develop the creative abilities of the rank-and-file employees.

DISCUSSION QUESTIONS

Has your organization used an employee suggestion or idea system in the past? If so, how would you characterize the program (for example, wide-open, complaint box, cost-savings contests, new product contests, or implemented improvements)?

What type of results did you experience?

Why is implementation by the proposer important to the success of a proposal?

6

From Untried Suggestions to Implemented Improvement Proposals

COMMON QUESTIONS ABOUT THE KAIZEN TEIAN APPROACH

The poster shown below was put up by a company to inform employees that it was switching from the old "request for ideas" system to a system based on implemented continuous improvements at the workplace. A company might give the following reasons for making this switch:

INVITING ALL EMPLOYEES TO PARTICIPATE IN KAIZEN PROPOSAL ACTIVITIES

SHARE YOUR SUCCESSFUL IMPROVEMENTS WITH OTHERS!

Employee proposals submitted after the second quarter of this year should be original creative ideas that were *successfully implemented* by the inventor. Please show concrete examples (with illustrations, labeled examples, and so on).

Note: Proposals submitted as ideas are no longer acceptable.

Deadline for submissions: _____

---

1. Under the idea request system, most suggestions recommend changes in other departments. Only a small percentage — about 1 or 2 percent of these suggestions — are ever implemented.
2. The old system is overburdened with suggestions that are studied and never realized; this is a big waste of time, and it lowers employee confidence and morale.
3. We spend a lot of time and money trying to promote improvements and make the present system work, but so far the results have not matched our efforts.
4. We have achieved employee participation already and see steady growth in suggestion activity. From now on, we need to promote better communication between supervisors and their employees with respect to proposals. We also want to promote proposal activity that will have an educational function and serve as on-the-job training. This is why we must embark on a new track with a system in which the proposer implements his or her kaizen ideas.
5. We need a system that transfers to the job site the responsibility and authority for reviewing proposals and providing guidance. In this system, each department will have the responsibility and authority to implement its own proposals.

When a company changes course and adopts a system of implemented improvement proposals, some controversy is inevitable. The following questions often arise:

1. It is natural to improve your own work as part of the job. Why should you receive bonus awards for that?
2. Why is it necessary to submit a written proposal for an improvement that has already been implemented?

3. How do I recognize the dividing line between my basic job responsibilities and my duty to make creative improvements in the workplace?
4. Shouldn't we consider suggestions from other departments?
5. What shall we do about proposals for development of new products and ways of doing business?

"Official Policy" Is Getting Nowhere

The next sections address these concerns.

QUESTION 1: ISN'T MAKING IMPROVEMENTS A PART OF THE JOB?

Bonus Awards Are a Means to Promote Improvement Activity

"Isn't it only natural to continually improve your job? That's a duty that comes with the job." This argument is often heard, and of course, the reasoning behind it is valid.

On the other hand, is this concept really put into practice? Do workers at your company make improvements as a matter of course, the way they carry out their other job responsibilities? If so, your company must be an ideal place to work.

In most companies, however, some employees keep improving their personal performance on the job without talking about it, and some also come up with improvement ideas. But the majority of employees tend to do the job the way it has always been done, to avoid complications.

It does take a lot of energy to change the way a job is done, to make an innovation, no matter how small it is. Often, people do not appreciate innovations — this is especially true of senior employees who are set in their ways.

Trying to make a change takes a lot of thinking, scrutinizing, negotiating, persuading, begging, and petitioning. And the result is not always what you had hoped for. If your proposal interferes with someone else's interests or places a supervisor in an awkward position, it may be rejected as inept, even if it is a good idea.

After meeting with enough of these obstacles, it is not surprising that people begin to think that innovations are not necessary, that things are all right as they are. People want to avoid conflict, so they tend to take the path of least resistance, which means upholding the status quo. Only when proper measures are taken to break down established customs and promote innovative activities will there be a general effort to bring about the changes that are inherent in continuous improvement.

Developing Creative Capabilities and Fostering the Desire to Improve

If you work for yourself and make independent decisions, it is a challenge to be innovative and exciting to overcome obstacles. Unfortunately, employees who work as part of an organization tend to become complacent and set in their ways. This complacency works against any effort to break down established patterns of behavior and to introduce creative solutions.

But if a business wants to beat the competition, it must unlock the creative potential of all employees and allow them to develop their capabilities in full. It must create a climate conducive to continuous improvement, even if it means paying special bonus awards for innovative proposals.

It is ideal when employees generate innovative proposals without a system and without the incentive of a bonus. But that is exactly what it is — only an ideal. A company does not live by its official policies and ideals alone. It exists in the real world. And in the real world of today, every company has to promote continuous improvement — it simply has no other choice. Modern corporations must have an official policy that acknowledges that workplace improvements are appropriate and therefore deserve a bonus. Such awards must be a part of the system, together with other mechanisms to promote continuous improvement activities.

QUESTION 2: WHY SUBMIT A WRITTEN PROPOSAL FOR AN IDEA THAT IS ALREADY IMPLEMENTED?

Creating a Positive Climate on the Job

One of the principles controlling our world is the "2-6-2" rule. According to this statistical principle, in any group of ten people there will be two who have very positive attitudes and will be full of enthusiasm. Another two people in this group will be very uncooperative and will oppose anything. The remaining six will be typical of the general majority, having no particularly positive attitudes but not being uncooperative. This middle group can be swayed in either direction, depending on the atmosphere and climate around them. The overall position of the entire group of ten will shift, depending on how the middle group is influenced.

Some 20 percent of employees (the positive-attitude group) will usually think about innovative changes, whether a proposal system is in place or not. Another 20 percent will never come up with any innovation, no matter how often they are urged to do so. The remaining 60 percent will participate in creative continuous improvement if a system for doing so is in place.

Continuous improvement activity is in fact a bottom-up management technique designed to push those 60 percent of employees off the fence so that they will participate and develop themselves. The emphasis on the terms *corporate culture* and *corporate climate* in recent years indicates that corporations are making an effort to influence the conduct patterns of the undecided 60 percent of its employees. It is that 60 percent that determines the base level of a corporation's performance.

The top 20 percent will develop their capabilities one way or another in any type of company organization. They are ambitious and they themselves want to excel, which is what makes them stand out. The 60 percent of employees in the middle need more prodding. If you want to set them in motion and bring out their potential, you have to create a system that motivates everyone and that builds innovative activity into the corporate climate. An improvement proposal system is one such mechanism. Ideally, 100 percent of employees should participate in this movement; at a minimum, the system should draw in the top 20 percent plus the 60 percent in the middle.

The main purpose of bottom-up management methods is to motivate the participation of the 60 percent in the middle

Creating the Conditions that Promote Creative Improvements

How do you motivate this 80 percent of employees to make creative improvements on the job? It is not enough to make loud announcements urging everyone to "please be innovative."

If employees ask "what is the scope of the innovations that we should bring up?" or "what should we be improving and how should we go about it?" most managers would be unable to answer because the conditions for promoting innovations have not been created.

This is the purpose behind the requirement that every improvement idea of every employee should be submitted in written form. Only after something is written down as a proposal can someone else understand the actual conditions of the workplace and the improvement that was made. This requirement clearly distinguishes departments that promote creative ways of doing the work from ones that maintain the status quo.

QUESTION 3: WHERE DOES THE REGULAR JOB END AND KAIZEN ACTIVITY BEGIN?

Creative Improvement Means Changing the Method

Many people believe that it is too difficult to distinguish the boundary between their regular job responsibilities and those involving creative improvement. If innovation is a part of their work, they reason, it should not merit a special bonus.

The problem with this line of reasoning is that it confuses the objective of a job with the method. The task and objective that you must achieve in your workplace, wherever it may be, is assigned to you in the form of job instructions. For instance, if you work in the sales department, your objective is to produce a certain amount of sales.

But there are a number of methods you can use to achieve this objective. Although some workplaces and occupations specify the method in the form of operational standards, in other types of occupations the method is left up to the worker to determine.

If the method of work is not rigidly prescribed, you can come up with many innovations by changing the method used to achieve your job objective. For example, you might change the way sales campaigns are conducted to make them more efficient, use a more effective operating method, use a more accurate office procedure, or work with safer tools. If you change the method, you are making creative improvements.

Kaizen means devising improved means and methods

A continuous improvement proposal movement is an activity that requires every employee to come up with a method or devise a mechanism that will help the company reach its goals faster and with more accuracy, so that work is safer, more enjoyable, and more productive. Any change that increases efficiency is a significant improvement and deserves praise.

A proposal system is meant to stimulate and promote this creative improvement activity. Unless such a movement is launched, the majority of employees will not risk creating tension by changing the way things are done. This is a big loss for both the company and its employees.

Even in an environment that is constantly changing, it is probably not necessary to seek change for its own sake. But when major factors such as competitors and affiliates change, old methods may prove ineffective and innovation will be necessary.

With some jobs, all that matters is the achievement of business results, and no one asks how things got done. In this type of job, workers have a free hand with respect to how they get a job done. Since they control the process, they are free to use whatever method they want, as long as they get positive results.

In today's environment, however, businesses can no longer carry on as if results were the only thing that mattered. They have to find out what it is that brings about good results and use this knowledge to integrate creative improvement into their working process. Rather than setting new norms telling workers how to do their job, they need to focus their attention on promoting kaizen activities.

Unfortunately, there are still too many companies that adhere to outmoded traditions despite calls for innovation.

QUESTION 4: SHOULDN'T WE CONSIDER PROPOSALS FROM OTHER DEPARTMENTS?

As explained earlier, implementation of proposals submitted by workers outside the department is a rare occurrence. This is why many people feel that such proposals should be prohibited.

In companies switching from a system of general proposals to a kaizen system, quite a few people may resist the change. They will complain that management should use the system to listen to the "voice of the people." They believe that management should reflect the opinions of its employees in its policy and should thus pay more attention to what the employees say. Even if they recognize that this type of system when put into practice is inefficient and ultimately lowers morale, they are still drawn by the theory behind the system.

To be sure, it is difficult to throw out a system in which people can freely speak their minds to higher-ups, even if only to let off steam.

Many companies have achieved a synthesis of the two systems, and to good advantage. This might be fashioned as follows:

1. Proposals are usually concentrated on creative improvements in a person's own work and they relate to implemented improvements.
2. The company accepts proposals that apply to other departments or to the company at large only during certain periods of the year.

This approach is the most rational for the following reasons:

- Since people do their jobs every day, they can improve their jobs every day as well. Therefore, they can make improvement proposals every day as a routine matter.
- When opinions, demands, and ideas for other departments and the company in general are gathered periodically, it is easier to actually listen to people's ideas about how the company is run; this is to everyone's advantage.

One of the problems with the old system of general proposals is that many of the proposals are similar and keep coming up again and again. This places the supervisor in the receiving department in the position of having to repeatedly explain why the proposal cannot be implemented, which is sure to be an annoyance as well as a waste of time.

Is it wise to hang on to a system so inefficient that it borders on the absurd? Companies that try to improve efficiency by these methods are in for a lot of trouble.

It is impossible for managers to hear out every proposal, opinion, demand, or idea, let alone try to implement all of them. It would mean that the company would stop functioning. This is why department heads must be given the responsibility to sort out the proposals and select some of them for action, even though this selection will inevitably be somewhat biased.

Limited periods for accepting proposals for other departments and the company in general

When certain times are designated for collection of proposals, reviewers can make categories of problem types. Such a breakdown reveals the problems that are of concern to a majority of employees. Thus it becomes apparent which problems have the highest priority and which proposals should be implemented. This is a more accurate way of finding out what is on the employees' minds than collecting isolated suggestions over a long period of time. Once the seriousness and priority are established, it is naturally much easier to decide which ideas should be carried out. This is a clear improvement over the old system, in which only trivial and useless proposals were carried out while important ones were postponed.

QUESTION 5: HOW DO WE DEAL WITH PROPOSALS FOR DEVELOPING NEW PRODUCTS AND NEW BUSINESS?

Development of new products and new ways of doing business is a topic that always comes up when proposal systems are discussed. Much of its popularity is due to media attention given to stories about the subject — how new employees have hatched new product ideas, how suggestions from checkout clerks made it possible to sell out the merchandise, and the like. People like to talk about how the company is soliciting ideas and plans from its employees for "new ways of doing business in the twenty-first century."

The popular attention given to ideas for new products and new business is one method for increasing conscious and active participation of employees, and it also enlivens the atmosphere, which is a good thing. For example, some companies have sponsored large-scale events in this vein. Toyota's Idea Olympics and Honda's Idea Contest were among them. These special events allow employees to forget the daily routine and express themselves in a creative way.

You should guard against placing too much importance on this endeavor, however. A company cannot be steered solely by accidental inventions and ideas. When they occur, they make big news, but it would be unwise to base plans on the expectation of a repeat performance. Despite their popular appeal, instances in which employee ideas have translated into big profit for the company are rare. In the real world, few managers give serious consideration to the grand schemes of their subordinates.

First Determine the Direction, Then Look for Proposals

You might think it narrow-minded to set limits on proposals, as such a step might inhibit the flow of fresh ideas from amateur inventors. It is certainly true that ideas from amateurs, who are looking at things from an optimistic perspective, can be much more interesting than the entrenched (and sterile) ideas of professional developers. Unfortunately, imagination alone does not create financial profit. Although imagination is vital, you also need a technique to convert this imagination into profit.

Ideally, the imagination of the amateur serves as the basis for professional product development techniques that will turn this imagination into financial gain. In real life, this is usually how success is achieved — except that the media, of course, focus on the amateur's role.

In this context, the role of a proposal system in activities such as new product and new business development becomes more evident. The system should require the professionals to create a solid foundation for new product development, while it expressly sets aside a role for amateurs to add new flavor and perspective through their proposals. There is a good possibility that this approach can lead to real breakthroughs. But unless a foundation and a direction are there, the chances of an amateur's good idea leading to a hit product are about as good as a person's chances of winning the lottery.

This is why the company should first establish a direction, making it clear that "this is the topic on which we are seeking ideas." It should also create a system for evaluating and implementing these ideas. New product ideas should be collected within a designated time period, and they should be placed in a category separate from continuous improvement proposals relating to daily tasks. A system that accepts any type of proposal at any time is virtually useless.

Although ideas are a precious commodity, they are not the only thing that should be taken into account. Evaluating them

**Determining the Direction and Theme
for Product Development Proposals**

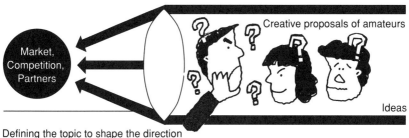

Defining the topic to shape the direction

and thinking them through should be just as important. The idea is like a seed that must be cultivated if it is to grow to maturity. People in production, distribution, operations, and sales need to understand that it is their collective effort that brings results.

DISCUSSION QUESTIONS

What concerns typically arise when a company adopts a system of implemented improvement proposals? How might these concerns be addressed?

PART THREE

How to Introduce and Manage
a Kaizen Teian System

How do you go about switching to kaizen teian activity that uses implemented improvement proposals from employees, and how should you manage this activity? A number of mechanisms and strategies are available. The following chapters suggest the "ingredients" that management should consider.

7

The Cycle of Kaizen Teian Activity

TRENDS AND KEY POINTS OF THE CYCLE

Kaizen teian proposal activity represents a cycle with four major components, shown in the figure on p. 100.

1. Persuading people to participate and work
2. Motivating them to write proposals (either implemented or unimplemented ideas)
3. Review, evaluation, and guidance
4. Award payments and commendations

If this cycle flows smoothly, the proposal activity will also run smoothly, one idea will lead to another, and continuous improvement will translate into improved productivity. On the other hand, if the flow is blocked at any of the key points, proposal activity will become irregular and the movement will begin to decline.

In short, proposal activity must be managed to ensure the smooth circulation of this flow. The first thing to consider when creating a proposal system and outlining its rules is, in fact, how

The Cycle of Teian Activity

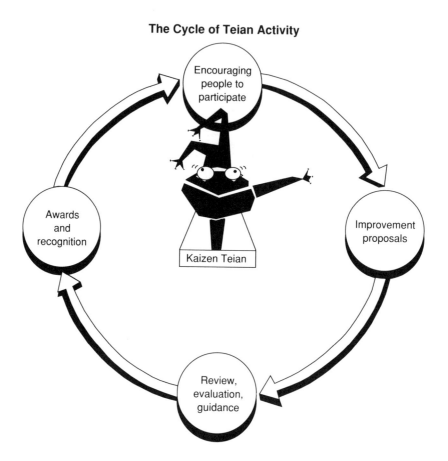

to make sure the cycle will run smoothly, without glitches. This should not be a big problem, provided that you have a blueprint of this cycle in your head.

If you do not grasp the whole picture, however, and simply imitate other companies' rules or management methods, you may end up with complicated regulations and create a lot of work for special review committees of one kind or another. To avoid a lot of troubles, remember that kaizen teian is different from other systems, and it need not be complicated.

Making improvement proposals is an activity that takes place on a daily basis in our jobs. That is why the system and its rules must be simple and easily applicable. After all, they are nothing but tools. The simpler the tools, the easier they are to use, and the fewer problems you will have.

If you just outline the fundamental principles, the systems will not be overly complicated. What you need is a system as simple and clear as possible.

Eliminating Causes of Problems

Even if you have already developed a proposal system, there will still be problems to deal with. Let's look at some measures that can help prevent the occurrence of problems. Specifically, you should think in terms of what is obstructing this cycle, then eliminate the causes of these obstructions.

Be careful not to take a measure simply because "they are doing it in company X." Even if another company is suffering from the same problem, such as a decline in the number of proposals submitted, the causes of obstacles to the flow of the cycle are often different, and so are the measures that should be taken. If the cause of the problem is that people do not understand the main purpose of and significance of writing proposals, you probably need to put more effort into informing and educating employees and creating a reference manual for that purpose. Employees probably also need training in how to write better proposals, and consulting and promotional team members need encouragement for their good work.

Finally, if progress is blocked by the awards that are paid, the bonus system must be reviewed and revised. Sometimes the system does not work because the award payments are too low; sometimes high awards create problems also. In any case, the award system must be modified to serve the activity's stage of development and level of maturity.

INFLUENCING PROPOSAL ACTIVITIES — PULL OR PUSH?

The methods for promoting and influencing proposal activity can be divided into two categories: "push" methods and "pull" methods.

Types of Push Strategy

The push strategy includes methods of influencing people from outside, nudging them in the desired direction of proposal activity. Some of these methods are soft and subtle, some are forceful and convincing.

Methods that use compelling measures, quotas, and targets will get positive results quickly, at least in the short term. They are definitely necessary in the initial period, until desired working habits have been established.

Campaigns and events, on the other hand, represent more subtle methods, a "soft" push. People naturally become interested when they see displays of improvement examples with positive results and when they can experience for themselves the meaning of continuous improvement. Such methods are helpful in shaping a public consensus about kaizen activities. You can achieve the participation of a large number of people in contests for posters, slogans, and so on, which is a very good strategy for getting across the meaning of achieving a higher level of involvement.

Other tools can also play an important role, such as articles on proposal activities in the company newsletter, reference manuals, notebooks, and so on. The latest technique at our disposal is company videos and other high-tech aids that help get people involved. Although we have developed a taste for high-tech techniques in our generation, this does not mean that older methods such as hand-made posters, leaflets, and similar aids cannot be effective.

The images of our time are often reflected in other items that can be used to promote proposal activity, such as flags, badges, and emblems. All of these can become useful tools for creating an atmosphere that is suitable for continuous improvement through proposals.

Using a Pull Strategy to Promote Involvement

In addition to these push methods, there is also a pull strategy. This typically involves encouragement or incentive offered by one person to another, or an employee getting a colleague involved in the activities.

One tool that can be used in this strategy is payment of bonus awards. Even if the awards are modest, it is better to have some payments than none at all. Small as they are, they will provide some money for refreshments or incidental expenses.

It is a common misconception that low awards are the reason for a low proposal rate. In reality, the opposite is true — if you raise the awards, fewer proposals will be made. Statistical data have confirmed that companies with the lowest bonus award payments have the highest level of kaizen teian proposal activity.

People who are concerned with the amount of award payments may still be thinking in terms of suggestion boxes and "money for ideas." If you accept this idea, then you are resigned to paying high amounts, as are typically paid in European and American systems. But kaizen based on a diametrically opposite concept. You improve your own job, and the subject of improvement is the work that you know better than anybody else. That is why the lower the award, the easier it is to come forward with a proposal. Even if they are only very small improvements, modest proposals can still be made without hesitation, one at a time.

People may say things like "I don't need any award to write an improvement proposal. I am doing it just because I want the company to do what I think is right," or "I don't care how much the bonus is, as long as you people listen to what I have to say." In truth, however, most people like a monetary award and will willingly accept one.

Proposal activity based on continuous improvement uses bonus awards as one component that makes the pull strategy more attractive. The award represents a recognition of a person's ideas. In this respect, it is clearly an important component of the strategy.

The other important pull components of proposal activity are review, evaluation, guidance, and, most of all, assistance with implementation. This combination of methods represents a powerful force that is instrumental in getting everybody involved.

When people talk about ways to promote proposal activities, they tend to concentrate on the push methods. These methods are very important, but if you want the promotion to succeed, don't forget to include the pull methods as well, plain and sober as they may seem. Otherwise, the channels may become clogged, the flow of proposals will stop, and no amount of work will make the system run as it used to.

If pushing doesn't work, try pulling!

REVIEW AND GUIDANCE ARE VITAL
TO PROPOSAL ACTIVITY

The biggest stumbling blocks in the proposal cycle lie in the area of review, evaluation, and guidance. When people submit their ideas for evaluation and never hear back from the examiners, they feel dejected and frustrated. The evaluators themselves soon get fed up with the mountain of proposals piling up on their desks, proposals that are never decided on one way or the other.

Insensitive comments of proposal reviewers can sometimes kill an employee's improvement initiative. Even if the evaluator means no harm in a written answer, if his or her intent is not communicated clearly, it invites negative misinterpretations.

When the review, evaluation, and guidance aspect of the system functions properly, it can be a great motivating force that will attract many excellent proposals. This force is clearly more effective than money awards or campaign appeals from management to come up with proposals. That is because the writer is primarily interested in getting his or her improvement proposal examined, recognized, evaluated, and, most important, implemented. Proposal activity will never function properly when this component of the process is neglected. This is the most important part of the innovation process.

Even when the mechanism of proposal activity has been created, and a proper strategy is in place to make this mechanism work, the system is not complete without appropriate approaches to the review process and the payment of awards.

Many companies have honest intentions of developing a proposal system for promoting implemented improvements but cannot relinquish the trappings of the old system — the direct appeals, complaint boxes, and conventional rules and evaluation methods. Even when modern principles and review methods have been adopted, the system itself remains fundamentally unchanged because the people enforcing the rules persist in treating proposals according to their own preconceived ideas. The new way may sound strange or illogical to them, so they attempt a counteroffensive. They take the attitude that "this is just another of those fancy theories the big shots came up with" or that "they don't really mean for us to actually carry it out." You may hear such statements from people who find it difficult to understand the new era that we live in. To keep them from reversing the momentum of the proposal system, you must find a way to erase these people's doubts, once and for all.

WHO SHOULD REVIEW THE PROPOSAL?

Supervisors Know the Work and the Worker

"Now that the number of proposals is growing, we can't keep processing all of them centrally. We will have to delegate the authority to process them to the section manager or the department manager." This is another comment frequently heard from corporate suggestion offices.

The problem here is that proposals should never be reviewed centrally in the first place. They should be examined by the person in charge of the workplace, right there on the spot. The supervisor or foreman is the one who knows the workplace better than anybody else. He or she knows about potential problems and where difficulties are likely to be encountered. In addition, the supervisor also knows the proposal writer better than anyone, since the employee reports to him or her.

A supervisor who sees the employees every day, who shares their problems and duties on the job, is the best qualified person to accept, review, and evaluate their proposals. Why? Because it is this supervisor who will have to approve the plans and provide the guidance required to make job improvements in connection with workplace problems anyway. This is also the best kind of on-the-job training available.

Examining Proposals Where They Are Made

In the kaizen teian system, the review authority belongs with the supervisor from the start. The idea of a centralized review process is a holdover from the days of suggestion or complaint boxes, when workers had to skip the direct supervisor to be heard.

With proposal systems based on work improvements and implemented proposals, however, the situation has been corrected. Workers are not forced to avoid the direct supervisor if they want to suggest something. On the contrary, things they notice every day on the job are food for thought. They can discuss their ideas with the supervisors, who will sit down with employees to resolve problems and put good ideas to work. This is the essence of proposal activity based on implemented improvements.

Responsibility for proposals that can be resolved on the spot should be gradually delegated to the place it belongs — the workplace. This is a great motivator for workers and it helps transform improvement activity into a system of implemented ideas.

HOW SHOULD THIS EXAMINING BE DONE?

The review of a proposal should be conducted fairly and promptly, in accordance with impartial evaluation standards. Many good examiners have gone through agony trying to meet these conditions. The problem is that reviewers cannot fulfill them all at the same time. It is impossible to be both prompt and impartial for every proposal that is submitted.

So how should proposals be reviewed? Different types of ideas call for different types of approaches.

Three Principles of Proposal Evaluation

Minor Proposals Should Be Evaluated Promptly

Promptness has top priority when it comes to minor proposals. It is not necessary to apply very strict standards to minor proposals. The awards will be in the $10 range at most, and the content of the proposal will not be all that difficult. It would be silly to ask a lot of busy, well-paid people to deliberate at length on the fate of such a proposal. There is no need to split hairs.

What is important with such proposals is that they be considered and evaluated promptly. If the evaluation drags on for several months, it is insulting to finally give out the news that "It has been adopted and your award is $1." The person who wrote the proposal inevitably feels that someone is taking him or her for a fool.

If the top award for a proposal is $10 or less, the decision should be prompt and clear. The employee is probably well aware where his or her proposal falls in the range of awards.

Strict Criteria Should Be Applied to Major Proposals

When the potential bonus award for a proposal is $50 or more, reviewers must apply cautious, strict, and impartial evaluation standards. The payment of larger award amounts is not to be taken lightly; evaluators should take care to follow proper procedures.

The employee is usually well aware of the importance of this kind of idea. Expectations will be high. He or she will feel entitled to have the content of the proposal properly reviewed and evaluated.

If a proposal has wide scope and affects other departments as well, discussions should be held between reviewers and other interested parties and should continue for as long as necessary. Since major proposals are not submitted every day, it matters less if the evaluation takes some time.

FAIRNESS THROUGH STATISTICS

When authority for reviewing proposals is left entirely to the workplaces, evaluations are bound to be somewhat biased. The same idea submitted in different departments might get very different evaluations, depending on the subjective views of examiners and other varying conditions.

Delegating proposal evaluation to the workplace level welcomes independent review of each proposal in accordance with the situation in each particular workplace. Naturally, such evaluations are subjective, and this is not necessarily a bad thing.

This is not to say, however, that this subjectivity will always regulate itself fairly without management interference. Some reviewers are indulgent, while others are overly strict; this is only natural. But it would not be fair to leave some people at the mercy of very strict supervisors.

This situation can be solved only through management of the review process in every department on a statistical basis. A comparison of the distribution of implemented proposals among all departments and work areas will make it clear which reviewers tend to be too strict and which are overly tolerant.

Since there is not such a big difference in creative capability among people working in various departments, it is not unreasonable to expect equal distribution among departments. The goal is to maintain overall fairness on a long-term basis. Management can ensure such long-term consistency by comparing samples of proposals, forming groups to study how proposals are reviewed, or simulating proposal evaluations.

THE MEANING OF A MONETARY AWARD

Most types of proposal systems pay some kind of bonus award, but the concept of an award varies according to the type of system used. The Japanese term for such an award has three meanings:

- compensation given to communicate a proposal's effect
- a reward that serves as an incentive or encouragement for further development
- an award that expresses appreciation for participation

In a suggestion box system, where ideas are exchanged for money, the main concept behind the bonus award is compensation. In an implemented proposal system, however, the three meanings are combined.

The Different Dimensions of Proposals and the Significance of Award Payments

The figure on page 111 shows how a system of implemented proposals is applied to the company employees. The process, which is broken down into several levels, is designed to encourage participation, develop skills, and achieve results.

Level 0 (Zero Energy, Zero Interest, Zero Responsibility)

At level 0, no one really knows what kind of problems a department has. "We are just doing as we are told. Who knows what this all means? And who cares, anyway?" This is what people will say initially, and naturally, no proposals or creative improvements will emerge at this level.

Proposal Levels and the Meaning of Award Payments

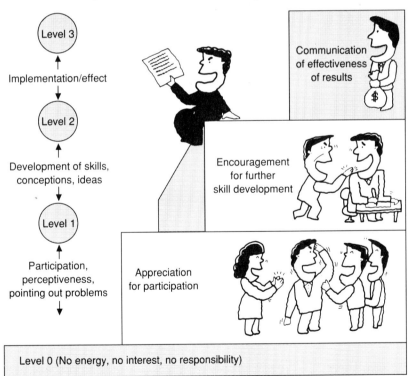

If people never moved beyond level 0, companies would be better off hiring robots. Robots never talk back, never get sick, and never need a vacation. But inevitably, people do move beyond level 0. Specifically, they notice problems and come up with interesting ways to solve them. This is why people should be expected to submit proposals.

Every job has two elements, maintaining existing conditions and breaking down existing conditions. At level 0, there is a lack of the second element, that is, of creative skills. This is a human characteristic that robots lack.

Level 1 (Noticing and Pointing Out Problems)

People must put all their energy into a job if they want to do it well. When there are problems, people should notice them and recognize that something should be done about them. But just knowing something and saying nothing is not enough. People need to point out the problems to others.

Although pointing out problems is not the same thing as making an actual improvement proposal, it is an important first step in creative improvement activity. In systems that rely mainly on "participation bonuses," it is the predominant level. At this level, the bonus awarded to an employee who points out a problem serves as a commendation.

Level 2 (Finding Causes of Problems, Raising Ideas, and Proposing Countermeasures)

At this stage employees are pointing out the problems and thinking about measures to cope with the problem. This process unfolds in several steps: Employees must find out what causes the problem, think up countermeasures, and then discuss those measures with their supervisors and colleagues. They must notice the material aspects of the problem, analyze them, and then restructure them into a solution. All of these actions strengthen their skills. Awards paid at this level serve as incentives to further develop those skills.

Level 3 (Making Decisions, Implementation, and Effects)

At this stage, several concrete countermeasures are studied, and decisions are made to accept or reject. Once accepted, the proposals are implemented, take effect, and either alleviate or solve the problem. This level of effort is awarded by payments that "inform" the employee that his or her creative effort had a positive conclusion. The award also informs others about this development.

DOES QUALITY COME FROM QUANTITY?

Many people seem to believe the myth that quality is borne of quantity. This same popular belief is behind a Japanese saying that assumes that a mountain with a broad base will also be high. According to this logic, the more proposals you have, the better your chances of receiving higher quality proposals.

These notions are not based on reality. The fact is, in systems encouraging a great number of proposals, those of medium and high quality will taper off, while those of low quality, the kind that will bring in only a "participation award," will grow. When management asks for "suggestions of any kind" in an attempt to pull in as many proposals as possible, people will expend more energy on writing proposals than on creative thinking and work.

This is not to say that there is no relation between quantity and quality, or that receiving a small number of proposals guarantees that they will be of high quality. The fact is, it is difficult to define *quality*. Most people agree that there is a relation between quality and quantity, but there is no such agreement on what constitutes high-quality proposals.

Executive managers and proposal system promoters give various answers when asked what determines the quality of a proposal. A good proposal, they say, is one that

1. is effective
2. has a wide range of applications
3. can be implemented
4. has already been implemented
5. represents a major idea
6. is "ingenious"
7. eliminates causes of problems
8. corresponds to the policy goals of the company
9. solves problems that affect all employees
10. does not cost a lot of money

This is not an exhaustive list by any means. If there is no agreement on the meaning of a quality proposal on the side that sends the message, how can employees on the receiving end understand what is wanted of them?

The Quality of a Proposal Is Determined by the Fulfillment of Objectives

When the objective of the proposal activity is simply effectiveness or good results, then the quality in a proposal means simply that the proposal is effective, saving big costs or making big profits.

But in a movement that strives for creative improvement proposals, "results" are not the only objective. Proposal systems of different companies are bound to serve different objectives. But most aim to promote participation (thereby energizing the workplace), development of skills (thereby creating employees that think), and effectiveness.

The quality of a proposal can thus be evaluated by the degree to which it fulfills those objectives. This evaluation takes into account the three levels mentioned earlier:

- the level of noticing (pointing out the problem)
- the conceptual level (suggesting countermeasures)
- the extent of the effect

You cannot improve the quality of proposals, then, by simply asking for more high- and medium-level proposals. Rather, you have to (1) encourage people to submit low-level proposals through participation bonuses, and (2) work to turn low-level proposals into medium-level ones to build a movement with truly creative proposals. Furthermore, you do not do this by simply encouraging people loudly and frequently; you must give workers a chance to practice creative improvement activities every day on their jobs.

Although participation bonuses figure only on the level of discovering and pointing out problems, once problems are defined, appropriate countermeasures can be adopted little by little. In this activity, the seed of creative improvement has been planted. If you cultivate this seed carefully, in due time it will bear fruit.

Only Education and Guidance Can Turn Quantity into Quality

Education and guidance are the agents by which quantity turns into quality. For example, during the initial stage, the guidance and assistance of supervisors and managers is indispensable. It improves communication, energizes the workplace, gives people incentives, and strengthens their motivation.

This also happens to be a very good form of on-the-job training for the workers, provided that proposals are submitted on a continuous basis. When proposals are submitted sporadically throughout the year, it is impossible to use this activity for OJT. Regardless of the kind of workplace, there must be at least one proposal submitted per month (or more often, depending on the job).

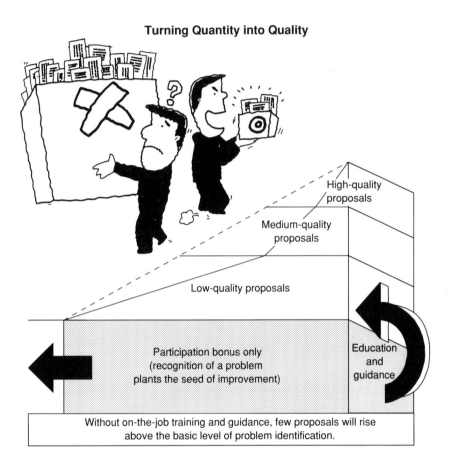

Turning Quantity into Quality

High-quality proposals

Medium-quality proposals

Low-quality proposals

Participation bonus only (recognition of a problem plants the seed of improvement)

Education and guidance

Without on-the-job training and guidance, few proposals will rise above the basic level of problem identification.

On the other hand, although quantity is important, a good education tool is created only when education and communication are included in the system. The employees are working on their jobs every day, so their progress also must be continuous and constant.

Keep in mind, however, that without guidance and education, there is no guarantee that quantity will turn into quality. Without this dimension, at a certain point — when there are too many proposals to deal with — quantity begins to translate into lower quality.

In the first stage of proposal activity, to get people in the habit of participating, managers need to use a little external pressure to get people's hands moving. What they write is not so important at first as the act of writing. Once the pattern of activity is established and is then nurtured through guidance from the supervisors, higher-quality improvement ideas will start to emerge.

"Only I Can Make My Own Head Think"

You cannot assure high-quality ideas by simply leading employees' hands. You must also get them to think. But you cannot do this by applying external pressure. Rather, you must first move their hearts, that is, give them the understanding and motivation to pressure themselves into making continuous improvement.

Even when a person is willing and motivated, this does not guarantee that you can simply request "better proposals." It is also necessary to develop the skills that make it possible for that person to think about improvements and to submit creative improvement proposals.

Persuasion, campaigning, and other forms of external pressure are useless in getting better proposals. This can be achieved only through the unfailing effort of the proposer, and through improvement skills that must be developed. Even when workers are willing to engage in improvement activity, unless they understand the rules and principles of continuous improvement, their efforts will be fruitless.

You cannot teach people the principles and rules of improvement by giving them difficult books to read and asking them to study hard. Instead, allow them to make improvements on the job, because continuous improvement is a skill acquired through frequent practice.

Setting proposal activity in full swing means moving the hands, hearts, and minds of workers. This cannot be achieved in

Moving hands, hearts, and heads

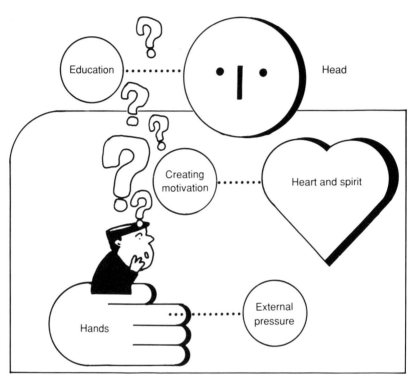

Sometimes pressure and encouragement are needed to get employees to start writing proposals. Once they acquire the habit of writing, it takes encouragement and training from management to produce high-quality proposals.

a single leap. Each step is necessary — from setting hands in motion to setting minds in motion.

IS HORIZONTAL DEPLOYMENT NECESSARY?

Horizontal deployment is often interpreted as the application of an idea from one department to other departments so that it will be utilized effectively. In reality, however, this deployment does not work as expected. Many people want to know what they can do to develop kaizen teian effectively in other departments. Ultimately, it is not really necessary for kaizen *ideas* to be deployed horizontally. The reason is simple: We are not talking about deploying isolated ideas but about spreading the development of improvement capabilities through all areas of the company.

This is like the issue of what kind of help should be provided to a developing country. Should such a country be given food, or should it be given assistance and guidance in the form of technology that will enable its people to grow food? If you give someone a fish, he or she will simply eat it and then it will be gone. But if you provide the fishing gear and the know-how, that person will be able to catch the fish independently from that moment on.

Trying to develop kaizen teian by imposing a few small improvements through all the departments is like offering one fish at a time. The more you are offered things in this manner, the more you are likely to lose motivation to make creative improvements on your own. Employees need to learn "how to fish" — how to apply kaizen teian principles to their own work.

Proposal Activity that Develops Skills

Since every department and workplace has its specific problems, the only people who can find the right solutions to these problems are those who work in those departments. Even though an improvement idea from another department may be similar, no two departments are identical; many ideas no longer apply when the conditions are different, even if the difference is small.

It would be a mistake to think that a few good kaizen ideas must be deployed in other departments across the board. Depending on the magnitude of the problem, each department must develop its own corresponding improvements. This is what gives significance to kaizen teian activities as a skill development measure.

Kaizen activity must certainly be put into effect in every department. If the ideas themselves must be implemented in other departments, this is best done through formal operating standards and work instructions, which must be enforced. This does not, however, devalue the importance of compiling, distributing, or displaying examples of creative improvements. Simply introducing kaizen examples and ideas will not achieve anything, however, unless you use this valuable material to develop motivation and improvement skills.

Examples can be put on display to convey the message that "you can achieve the same improvement" and that "we expect that in your department you will come up with an even more ingenious idea." Once people read the material, they will get the message. This approach is much more effective than direct appeals for creative improvements.

How to Handle Similar Proposals

A related problem that often comes up is that of how to deal with similar proposals from different people. It is only natural that similar proposals will emerge from different departments when those departments suffer from similar problems. In fact, this occurrence is an indication of successful horizontal deployment of kaizen skills. This is a good thing! Consequently, managers should value and encourage such proposals.

A proposal is not a commodity that should be limited and protected — the idea is to encourage further creativity and originality. Good ideas from one department should be applied to other departments as well, and improvements from other companies can be also incorporated.

In the case of similar proposals, however, review committees do not necessarily reach identical conclusions. The degree of urgency will differ in different departments. When the gravity of problems varies in different workplaces, it is only natural that the evaluations given to proposals will differ as well.

WHAT MAKES A GOOD IDEA?

You sometimes hear the comment: "It's a great idea, but unfortunately, we can't implement it." This is a contradictory statement. If it cannot be implemented, by definition it is not a good idea. Ideas and proposals that cannot be implemented are about as useful to a company as is a picture of a delicious meal to a hungry person. The idea becomes valuable only when it has been implemented and becomes a reality. So the comment mentioned above really means "it *would* be a great *if* it could be realized."

Take for example the following proposition: "Let's double everyone's salaries." There is no doubt that it would be a wonderful thing to do; unfortunately, most companies lack the capital and concrete means that would make it possible.

A proposal must be more than mere wishful thinking and idealism. What is needed are concrete methods that turn wishful thinking into implemented ideas. This essential component must be in the proposal. If it is absent, it cannot be called a good proposal.

Costly Proposals Are Hard to Implement

When people say, "That's a good idea, but we can't implement it," they usually mean that it is too costly or risky, that it would not work well in the system, or that it has some other limitation. The worst limitation is probably excessive cost. One reason proposal review takes a long time is that the reviewers have to establish whether implementation would be expensive. Many projects could be implemented easily, but they would cost a lot of money. Since every company has restrictions on its budget, company funds cannot be used to implement costly proposals and wishful thinking. Other things will always take priority.

That is why proposal activity must emphasize resourcefulness and ingenuity over great expense. This focus will result in proposals that can be put into practice easily. The most practical and effective methods are those that do not cost money, that are ingenious, and that can be easily realized.

Reviewers and administrative workers must make this concept very clear when commenting on proposals and encouraging employees to write up their ideas. Rather than simply saying, "If you have a good idea . . . ," say instead, "We are looking for practical ideas that can be implemented right away." It is essential to make very clear that a "good idea" means a proposal that costs as little as possible, and that only then is it a good proposal.

It was customary in the past for reviewers to offer polite commentaries on employees' proposals by way of encouraging them to write more proposals. There is no point, however, in

praising people and complimenting them on something that is of no use. This would not be a very responsible attitude.

To make best use of proposal writing, reviewers should be honest in their assessments. Otherwise, the proposal system will become a sham and lose all effectiveness. When supervisors and managers understand the purpose of proposal writing and guide the employees in making proposals that serve that purpose, then the activity becomes a valuable means of on-the-job training.

DISCUSSION QUESTIONS

What are the four major components of the kaizen teian cycle?

Name three "push" (external pressure) strategies for promoting participation in improvement activities.

Name two "pull" (encouragement) strategies for promoting participation.

Why should proposals be reviewed by the direct supervisor rather than a central authority?

Under the kaizen teian system, how can companies improve the quality of proposals?

What constitutes a "good idea"?

How should reviewers respond to poor proposals?

8

Evaluation Standards: Simple Rules for Quick Decisions

RULES AND STANDARDS FOR MODERN COMPANIES

Why does evaluation, the aspect that concerns the employee most of all and that is vital for proposal activity, so often hinder the development of this activity? The following reasons are commonly found:

1. The evaluation standards are too complex.
2. Proposals are not reviewed and evaluated quickly enough.
3. On proposals that have been quickly reviewed and evaluated, no decision is made.
4. Too many important aspects must be taken into account.

That is why employees too often hear the response that their proposals are "being reviewed" or that "someone is looking at it." This usually means that even perfectly functional and useful ideas are simply piling up on someone's desk. In this age of rapid change everywhere, companies can no longer make do with such sluggish methods. They must be able to solve problems right away; innovation that takes time is useless. They must review, evaluate, and make decisions on proposals on the day they are made; only then will they be able to energize their managerial strategy.

The types and styles of companies in business today are becoming diversified. The ratio of "soft" businesses such as services is increasing in relation to manufacturing. Proposal evaluation standards must be designed to reflect the diversity of the age. Companies with very active proposal movements have adopted flexible measures that respond to rapid changes. Companies whose systems are lagging behind the modern approach are quickly becoming obsolete. It is essential to use a system that is fast enough to meet requirements of the modern era — that evaluates proposals quickly, promptly determines adoption, and implements ideas. The most important characteristic of a continuous improvement proposal system is simplicity.

Evaluation Standards Must Match the Purpose

Many companies use evaluation standards like those shown on page 127. They often include evaluation points such as "efficiency," "novelty of ideas," or "effort." Each of these categories is assigned a certain number of points; the total score will determine the grade or class of the proposal and the corresponding award amount.

Unfortunately, this method is time consuming and confusing for reviewers. To give an example, even when reviewers gain a sense of the proposal's worth on first reading, they must still go through the motions of assigning the points to arrive at the grand total. Thus a proposal that they "know" should get only a minimal award will sometimes end up with a total that would garner a larger award. Then the reviewers must erase everything and waste time in another fruitless exercise to make the point total come out "right," trying to make the basic evaluation standards agree with the rating they think appropriate.

Old-style Evaluation Standards

Evaluation Factors	Principal Review Items and Evaluation Points			
	Very significant	**Considerable**	**Small**	**Not significant**
Effect (40)	40　38　36　34	30　28　26　24	20　18　16　14	10　6　4　0
Originality (25)	Highly novel and creative 25　23	Quite original, offering a wide sphere of application 20　18　16	Can be creatively applied with some help; creative when widely applicable 14　12　10　8	Similar examples elsewhere; not very creative or insightful, but has reference value 6　4　2　0
Effort (20)	Required a great deal of effort 20　18	Required quite a bit of effort 16　14　12	Required some effort 10　8　6	Just a lucky strike, very little effort 4　2　0
Possibility of implementation (15)	Can be implemented immediately 15　12	Requires a preparation period 10　8	Still some room for improvement and more thinking 6　4	Will require a lot of further study; hard to tell if proposal has much future 2　0

Class of proposal and award payment

Class	Points	Payment
Class 7	30 points or more	¥500
Class 6	40 points or more	¥1,000
Class 5	50 points or more	¥2,000
Class 4	60 points or more	¥3,000
Class 3	70 points or more	¥10,000
Class 2	80 points or more	¥20,000
Class 1	90 points or more	¥30,000

A partial solution to this problem is the "quick evaluation chart" shown on page 129. This is a simplified set of instructions explaining classifications of proposals and giving guidelines for using it.

This chart consists of three levels of evaluation, which correspond to the three objectives of a proposal:

- *Participation:* taking notice of problem areas
- *Development of skills:* generating innovative ideas for countermeasures
- *Effect:* getting results through implementation of the proposal

The Participation Objective

Participation consists in struggling with work-related problems. This is something every employee is capable of and should be expected to do. A proposal system is designed efficiently for this purpose. If such a system is to function properly, however, the object and manner of proposal evaluation must be defined.

The submission of a proposal usually indicates the following:

1. There is a problem.
2. Someone took notice of the problem and alerted others to it.
3. Someone came up with an idea for solving the problem.

Thus, a proposal indicates that the innovator is acting in a positive manner to solve work-related problems. Even if the process ends there, this participation should be appreciated.

There are, of course, various levels of participation. Participation is always influenced by prevailing attitudes in the workplace and in management. It can also be influenced by factors that the participants are unaware of. In such cases it is

Quick Evaluation Chart

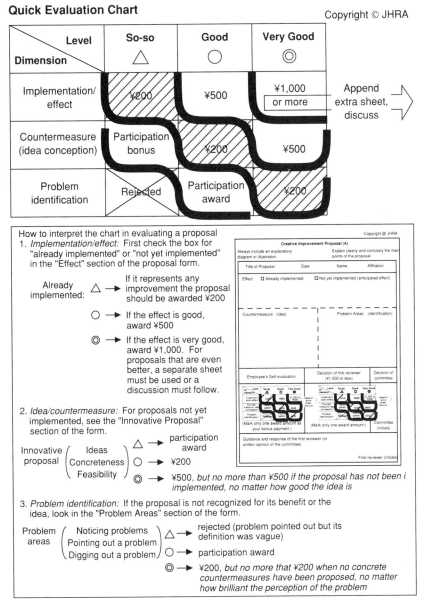

Level / Dimension	So-so △	Good ○	Very Good ◎	
Implementation/ effect	¥200	¥500	¥1,000 or more	Append extra sheet, discuss
Countermeasure (idea conception)	Participation bonus	¥200	¥500	
Problem identification	Rejected	Participation award	¥200	

How to interpret the chart in evaluating a proposal

1. *Implementation/effect:* First check the box for "already implemented" or "not yet implemented" in the "Effect" section of the proposal form.

Already implemented: △ → If it represents any improvement the proposal should be awarded ¥200

○ → If the effect is good, award ¥500

◎ → If the effect is very good, award ¥1,000. For proposals that are even better, a separate sheet must be used or a discussion must follow.

2. *Idea/countermeasure:* For proposals not yet implemented, see the "Innovative Proposal" section of the form.

Innovative proposal (Ideas / Concreteness / Feasibility)

△ → participation award

○ → ¥200

◎ → ¥500, *but no more than ¥500 if the proposal has not been implemented, no matter how good the idea is*

3. *Problem identification:* If the proposal is not recognized for its benefit or the idea, look in the "Problem Areas" section of the form.

Problem areas (Noticing problems / Pointing out a problem / Digging out a problem)

△ → rejected (problem pointed out but its definition was vague)

○ → participation award

◎ → ¥200, *but no more that ¥200 when no concrete countermeasures have been proposed, no matter how brilliant the perception of the problem*

Notes   1. The amount of the bonus and the level at which a bonus will be paid depends on the conditions at each company.
2. An immediate bonus should be paid for an implemented improvement and a dimension and level should be assigned to it.

especially valuable if these factors are pointed out in the form of a proposal.

The Skill Development Objective

While participation can mean simply pointing out a problem, skill development requires devising a solution to the problem, that is, making an improvement proposal.

"There's more than one way to skin a cat," as the saying goes. There are an infinite number of ways to solve a single problem, and solutions can be made on various levels. This level depends in part on the extent of

- the understanding of present conditions
- the effort to determine the causes of the problem
- the study of kaizen teian ideas and countermeasures
- the analysis of the potential effect of the implemented proposal

If you are able to see only the present circumstances, the countermeasures you design will correspond only to the circumstances that are obvious to you. If, on the other hand, you delve into the cause of a problem, you will be able to submit a creative proposal with countermeasures that will eliminate this cause.

Evaluation standards traditionally included the item called "original idea" under the category called "effort." This is because a high level of original thinking reflects and presumes investigation, research, study, and other activities that involve effort. Originality is also measured by structural factors such as the concreteness of the proposal and the possibility of implementation.

Certainly it takes ingenuity to come up with proposals that are as inexpensive as possible and that can be implemented as easily as possible. If there were no limits to the amount of time and money available, anything at all would be possible, but sheer originality is not by itself a measure of a proposal's worth. More important criteria in determining the level of originality in a proposal are concreteness and possibility of implementation. Only if these traits are present does a proposal express a high level of original thinking.

The Effectiveness Objective

The *effect* that we are evaluating is the substantial effect — tangible or intangible — of the proposal once it has been implemented. Only proposals that have been implemented can be evaluated for their effect.

The distinction between proposals that have not been implemented and those that have is reflected in the awards system. Payments made for "detection of problems" and for "originality" represent an *investment* in the training of talented employees, whereas payments made for "effect" are considered as *compensation* for the merit of the proposal.

The distinction is an important one. As said before, even a brilliant idea has no merit unless it is put to use. This is why proposals that have not yet been implemented should be evaluated only on their perceptiveness and creative thinking, not on their effect.

What the Level of a Proposal Means

The sections for the bonus payment guide in the quick evaluation chart are arranged in this order: (1) effect, (2) originality, and (3) detection of problems. These "dimensions" of a proposal are reflected in the evaluation.

Perceiving a problem has little value on its own, although *not* perceiving a problem is worse, signifying that the worker has not progressed beyond the level 0 mentioned earlier — the level characterized by lethargy, indifference, and irresponsibility.

For workers in level 1, the "detection of problems" level, the hope is that the same workers who noticed the problem will ask themselves how to fix the problem. Even if they submit only a crude proposal, they will have progressed to the next level, that of creative thinking. In a level 2 proposal, we are also evaluating a positive attitude and motivation, examining study and research activities, a necessary part of the process that hones problem-solving skills.

On the other hand, the best idea in the world cannot have any effect if it is not implemented. An implemented proposal — one that has an effect — is thus always on a higher level. To implement a proposal, the proposer must obtain permission from supervisors, and must persuade colleagues to cooperate or help. That requires a lot of effort and work and is another distinguishing factor between proposals that are untried and those that have been implemented.

The four levels of proposal activity were introduced in Chapter 7. The figure on page 133 describes the objectives and the meaning of the award payments, at each of these levels.

If all I do is notice things (and point out problems), I may be terribly clever, but I will earn no more than a participation award, around ¥100 (less than $1). If I also submit a proposal for improving the problem, whatever it is, the award is upgraded by one level to ¥200 or ¥500 (approximately $1.50 to $3). If this proposal is not implemented, however, my idea, clever as it is, can earn no more than ¥500.

Once an idea is implemented and has an effect, an award will be paid corresponding to the effect, such as ¥1,000 or ¥2,000 (approximately $6 to $12). If an implemented proposal has a major effect, the award payment may be larger. The precise amount of payment can be determined by standards prepared especially for these cases or through discussion among reviewers.

In any case, prompt action on proposals is the key to a successful improvement activity. If the review process takes too long, or has to be handled by some committee of "important" people, the improvement activity will never get off the ground. If a proposal has to go to a committee for first evaluation, the decision might come after the writer's job has changed. It is

Table for Evaluating Level and Objectives

	Level	Objective	Evaluated Item	Content of Evaluation, Level	Meaning of Award
0	Indifference Irresponsibility Lethargy				
1	Positive attitude Problem awareness	Participation	Problem identification	1. Noticing things (perceptiveness, identifying problems) 2. Dealing with problems on the job (dissatisfaction and complaints → formulation of problems) 3. Defining problems (phenomenon → cause)	Education and training of employees
2	Examining, research, ingenuity, planning, studying, devising solution	Skill development	Countermeasure idea	1. Ingenuity, ideas 2. Concreteness, ease of realization 3. Level of research, study, analysis (incidental idea → phenomenon and its cause → influence)	Investment Incentives
3	Implementation, consent, cooperation, followed by effect	Effect	Effect implementation	Tangible effect — Lower costs / Increased sales Intangible effect	Effect deserves compensation award as incentive

essential to implement useful creative improvement ideas as soon as possible.

There is no point in managers spending a long time deliberating whether a proposal should receive ¥500 or ¥1,000 (on the level of $3 to $6). For award payments of ¥1,000 or less, managers should make a quick decision, saving their time and energy to develop and implement people's ideas.

A PROPOSAL FORM THAT STARTS WITH THE EFFECT

In the sample proposal form shown on page 135, the first section to be filled in is entitled "Effect." This section is followed by other sections, titled "Originality (innovativeness, creativity)" and "Problem detection (observation)." Although it may seem to be arranged in reverse order, this form is used by many corporations.

There are several reasons for beginning the form with "Effect":

1. One of the basic rules of business is "start with the results." A proposal form is no exception to this rule.
2. It is natural to introduce a proposal by describing the effect it will have, since an intended effect is what prompts employees to write proposals.
3. The reviewer should know of this anticipated effect from the beginning. Then, he or she can use that as a basis for grading the proposal or providing further guidance.

The fact is that many proposals are organized in a way that makes them difficult to understand. Writers tend to focus on the background to the problem, arranging details haphazardly, chaotically intermixing description, interpretation, complaints, and suggestions. The reviewer is left hopelessly confused.

To begin with the anticipated effect, however, is to put all ensuing information into context. Once the anticipated effect is stated, the concepts of the proposal are easily explained in the

Creative Improvement Proposal (A)

Always include an explanatory diagram or illustration.

Explain clearly and concisely the main points of the proposal.

Title of Proposal	Date	Name	Affiliation

Effect   ☐ Already implemented   ☐ Not yet implemented (anticipated effect)

Countermeasure   (idea) | Problem Areas   (identification)

Employee's Self-evaluation	Decision of first reviewer (¥1,000 or less)	Decision of committee

(Mark only one award amount as your bonus payment.)

(Mark only one award amount.)

Committee (initials)

Guidance and response of the first reviewer
(or written opinion of the committee)

First reviewer (initials)

"originality" section, which follows. After these sections have been filled in, there is little need for a lengthy description of the problem itself. Another advantage to this form is its side-by-side placement of the problem and the proposed solution.

Using Self-evaluation for Efficiency

The proposal form includes two of the quick evaluation charts introduced on page 129. The first chart is completed by the employee, thus serving as a self-assessment of the proposed improvement. The initial reviewer then completes the second chart as part of the evaluation.

This aspect of the proposal form also has advantages:

1. It makes clear what the employee is suggesting
2. It expedites the process of review and guidance by setting out our reasons for writing it:
   - we want to point out a certain problem
   - we want to have our own ideas evaluated and adapted
   - we want others to acknowledge the effect of our improvement

All these concerns of the proposal writer should be taken into account and specifically evaluated by the reviewer. The reviewer should appraise each specific area of the proposal, since he or she has to respond to the proposal. If the employee's self-evaluation and the reviewer's evaluation are identical, there is no need for a detailed commentary. In such cases, the points that the employee wants others to acknowledge are clearly validated.

On the other hand, if there is a discrepancy between the self-evaluation and the reviewer's evaluation, some commentary and further guidance will be necessary. Even if the employee is convinced of the proposal's worth, his or her supervisor must still study factors such as its safety, its cost-effectiveness, and its influence on the next stage of the process.

Conversely, it is also possible that a proposal given little value by the employee will prove to be a great idea from which the entire company will benefit. This too requires commentary and specific feedback.

RULES FOR "BUSINESS IMPROVEMENT" PROPOSALS

Proposal systems can have several possible objectives, including

- product development and improvement
- establishment of a new enterprise
- improvement of an existing enterprise

Although the first two categories garner the most media attention, the third category in fact contributes the most to strengthening the corporate structure. True business improvement takes place through continuous daily implementation of small improvements at the employees' own worksite, using the creative ingenuity of each person.

To efficiently manage a proposal system, the management should make it clear which of the categories it considers most important. If it fails to do so, there will be differences of opinion among the people who promote the proposal activity, as well as among the rank-and-file employees. This will create unnecessary confusion and discontent.

While it is natural for different people to have different objectives, the result of these differences will be that regulations, standards, organization, and methods of management, which represent the means to achieve these objectives, will also differ.

One example of a strategy for clarifying the objectives of proposal systems is shown on page 139. This strategy has the following characteristics:

1. Improvement activity is considered part of a person's actual job and thus is expected of everyone.

2. The most important improvements are those made in a person's own job.
3. Implemented proposals should be promoted especially actively. Employees submit these to their direct supervisors, making them an occasion for on-the-job training.
4. Proposals for other departments are considered "reference proposals"; they are treated as useful only as a second opinion. This helps to prevent unnecessary disappointment and also saves time and labor.

How to Appraise a Reference Proposal

The "reference proposal" concept is a most important new approach. This is a response to the fact that proposals for other departments are the source of bottlenecks in the evaluation and implementation system.

Most conventional proposal systems are initially swamped by a large number of proposals for other departments. It is said that the spectators understand the game better than the players, and indeed, it is easier to see other peoples' errors than to see your own. That is why outsiders sometimes do come up with creative proposals that present fresh and original concepts.

The problem with this free-ranging approach is what to do once these ideas are collected. Submitting proposals is one thing, but someone has to review them and decide whether to use them. The reality is that most ideas submitted through such a proposal system will remain permanently "under review."

To stay competitive, however, companies should not ignore proposals from other departments. Rather, each department should actively gather information on a daily basis and remain open to various points of view, opinions, and ideas, which takes a lot of effort and energy. They should accept proposals from people working in other fields gladly and with gratitude, provided that these people are seriously trying to make work easier and more efficient.

Principles for a Creative Improvement Proposal System

1. Purpose

The main purpose is "to make my job and the work in my workplace better through creative improvements."

(1) Participation: Ingenuity and creative thinking are encouraged, and active participation is promoted.

(2) Skill development: Improvement proposals represent an occasion for "real life on-the-job training," and they help to develop skills.

(3) Effect: The aim is to create a workplace where working is easy, thus building a firm corporate constitution.

2. Object

(1) All employees should participate in improving the company; everyone should submit proposals.

(2) Everyone from the president to the line supervisors must promote improvement proposal activity. Providing guidance to others is an important job.

3. The Content and Types of Proposals

Every constructive proposal, even if it is a minor innovation, benefits the company. On the other hand, demands, grievances, and complaints that do not represent improvement proposals will be rejected.

(1) Implemented proposals: These are proposals that have been already realized and whose effect has been verified.

(2) Proposals not yet implemented: These are suggestions that are also considered proposals, although they have not yet been implemented (they are original concepts, innovative ideas, and accurate perceptions of problems that will be evaluated).

(3) Reference proposals: These are improvements proposed for the work of other departments. Needless to say, employees working in the department in question use them for reference. (If these proposals are recommended by employees working in the department in question, however, they deserve a special commendation.)

4. How to Submit Proposals

(1) In principle, proposals are submitted to the first reviewer (direct supervisor of your workplace). After obtaining guidance and permission, you should implement them whenever this is possible (these proposals will be classified as proposals that have already been implemented).

(2) You can also submit proposals directly to the corporate offices, but such proposals will be accepted only as reference proposals. The corporate offices are not responsible for examining, answering, or implementing such proposals.

5. Evaluation and Feedback

(1) Details regarding the reviewers, evaluation standards, the review process, and incentive awards are provided in a enclosure to this document.

(2) Reviewers are responsible for evaluation of proposals; they must respond to proposals and provide guidance.

6. Ownership of Rights

(1) Rights relating to the content of a proposal belong to the company.

(2) In case the right of industrial ownership is applied for, a separate application must be submitted in accordance with the job-related invention regulations.

Why

What

How

Proposals and opinions that come from outside the department represent valuable reference material and should thus be treated with great respect. On the other hand, the truth is that much of such material will not be useful even for reference; that accounts for the stock response of "We're looking into it."

It is probably also true that only when each department is able to resolve its own problems, is it in a good position to assess proposals from outside. Once it has reached this stage of proficiency, the department can develop new kaizen activities easily.

It is fine to be able to say anything to any other department, but unless improvement activity in one's own department is in very good shape, a person can hardly bring about progressive development in the company. This is one reason why kaizen activity encourages proposals that represent implemented ideas of company employees. Such an approach makes it obvious where the real emphasis of improvement activity should be.

No matter how modest a proposal may be, its implementation is a great boost for the morale of all the employees. This is an example of strengthening the corporate structure. To strengthen its position, a company must develop improvement skills in each department and create an atmosphere conducive to improvement activity.

Business improvement, which is the main target, can be achieved only if the improvement activity involves close cooperation between subordinates and their supervisors. It would be nonsense to create a system for submitting improvement proposals directly to a management committee, circumventing direct superiors. Moreover, a manager would be foolish to approve a proposal without first consulting the writer's supervisor.

On the other hand, bosses are human too, and they have their own prejudices and fixed ideas. It is important to have some mechanism to prevent the harm that could come from such behavior. One possible way is to maintain a system of direct appeal to upper management, but only as a supplementary system.

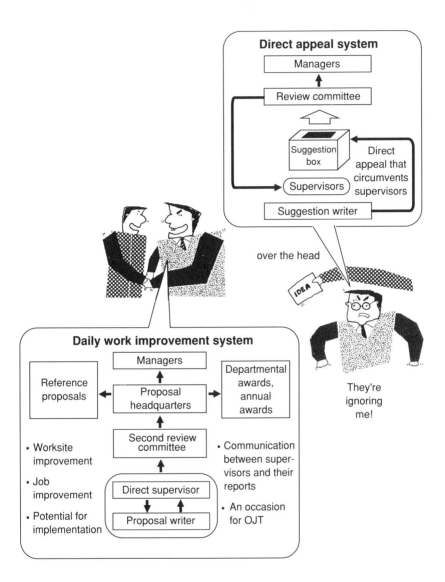

Rules and standards that are used in one corporation are not always applicable to another corporation. They must correspond to the actual state of things at each company. If there is any common denominator, it is to keep the rules of proposal activity simple so that people can refer to and use them easily.

DISCUSSION QUESTIONS

What problems are commonly found in evaluation systems that fail?

What are some of the strong points of a "quick evaluation chart"?

Why is it a good idea to make "Effect" the first section of a proposal form?

9

Examples of Implemented Improvement Proposal Activity

This chapter presents some examples of proposal forms and evaluation standards actually used in companies engaged in improvement activity.

PROPOSAL FORMS OF JR WEST JAPAN

The figure on page 144 shows the proposal form used by JR West Japan (a private company formerly part of Japan Railways). Revised in 1989, the form shattered conventional concepts of what proposal forms should look like. It has the following characteristics:

1. To avoid using the word *proposal*, which may be misleading, the company named this form a "Kaizen Sheet." In so doing, it emphasized the fundamental objective of the movement, which is kaizen, or continuous improvement.
2. The column entitled "Effect" appears at the top of the form. This is a concrete application of the business principle stating that "the report follows from the conclusion."

Kaizen Sheet

JR West Japan

No.:
Date received:

Title of Improvement	Type	Name and no.	
	Adoption Trial implementation Reference	Site and workplace	
		Submitted by (circle)	Individual group

Effect

• Describe concretely, specifying the value in financial terms, if possible.

Creativity means
work that is more fun

Implemented Improvement

☐ Implemented
☐ Not yet implemented

• Please explain on a diagram

Current Problem Areas

• List all the problems, using concrete examples. Were there complaints from passengers about indifference, irresponsibility, and lethargy?

Hint: The real cause of problems can often be best understood if you divide problems into their separate elements.

Kaizen Solution

• Should we drop something altogether or change a procedure?
• Use checklist for reference

Problems give you a chance to be innovative

Kaizen Review Chart

			Compensation (remuneration, incentive)		Kaizen Guidance, Response, Comment	Evaluation	Class
	So-so	Good	Very good	Corporate office			
Effect	Class 5 ¥500	Class 4 ¥1,000	⇒ Proposal adopted	Class 1 - Class 3			
	↑OJT	↑OJT	↑OJT				
Idea	Advice	Trial implementation ¥100	Trial implementation ¥100	Implemented (Y or N)			
	↑OJT	↑OJT	↑OJT				
Problem detection	Advice	Advice	Advice	Inquiry	Second Reviewer		(stamp)

Levels described as "so-so," "good," and "very good"
will vary, depending on the knowledge and abilities of
individual employees, and on their expertise.

3. The arrows direct one through the course of thinking about an improvement. Thus the form itself guides the writer. It can also be used for practicing innovative thinking and for evaluating an improvement from different viewpoints.

4. Essential points from the list of evaluation criteria appear with instructions on grading. This arrangement encourages the development of skills and promotes on-the-job training through improvement activity. The list can also be used as a self-grading checklist. Unlike the example shown on page 135, this form does not use parallel columns for two reviewers. It is simple to distinguish the entries of different reviewers, because their remarks and changes are made in a different color of ink.

5. Evaluation standards are based on the concept of education of the company's human resources, so that all employees can develop their professional knowledge and talent and can become practiced in innovative activity. The term "advice" is an important one in this connection.

The company's old proposal system, put in place when the company was still a government-owned railway, stressed proposals relating to other departments and to the company in general. As a result, an extremely small percentage of proposals ever got implemented. As soon as the company came under private management, however, it began studying new proposal systems, and after some experimentation, it adopted the new style of form.

EVALUATION STANDARDS FOR PROMPT DECISIONS AT TOYOTA

The figure on page 147 shows the evaluation standards used by the Toyota Motor Company. Although it is a very detailed set of criteria, one main point to note appears at the very top (see detail): "Except for proposals that are awarded 0 or ¥2,000 and over, the evaluation ratio should be 50 percent receiving ¥500 and 50 percent receiving ¥1,000." Point-based evaluation is not necessary. It also specifies that "proposals that are not yet implemented are awarded either 0 or ¥500."

Such points show the real power of Toyota, a leader in kaizen. The idea is that complicated calculations are no longer required for awards of ¥1,000 or less, which allows the reviewer to promptly assess a proposal on the basis of his or her own sense of its value. This regulation expresses the actual evaluation methods, not just a principle or policy.

Since the power to authorize awards of up to ¥1,000 is at the discretion of each department head, problems of fairness may arise. On the other hand, the reviewer is obliged to uphold the standard providing that 50 percent should get ¥500 and 50 percent ¥1,000. This in itself ensures a certain degree of fairness. It is this manager's responsibility to get a certain number of kaizen proposals from the employees. If an employee was consistently singled out for low awards, he or she would soon stop writing, which would reflect badly on the manager. This prospect helps avoid bias in the process.

In addition, a proposal that has not yet been implemented will receive only ¥500 at most, no matter how splendid the idea. This rule makes it clear that an idea is valuable only once it has been put to work.

Award Money Criteria		equivalent to			
Points received	C 0-4	B 5-7	A 8-9	10-11	12-14
Award money 10,000s of yen	none	.05	.10	.20	.30

• Except for proposals that are awarded 0 or ¥2,000 and over, the evaluation ratio should be 50 percent receiving ¥500 and 50 percent receiving ¥1,000.
• Proposals that are not yet implemented are awarded either 0 or ¥500.

Award Money Criteria

Points received	equivalent to			10-11	12-14	15-17	18-20	21-23	24-26	27-29	30-32	33-35	36-38	39-41	42-44	45-46	47-48	49-50	51-52	53-54	55-56	57-58	59-61	62-64	65-67	68-70	71-73	74-75
	C 0-4	B 5-7	A 8-9																										
Award money 10,000s of yen	none	.05	.10	.20	.30	.40	.50	.60	.80	1.0	1.5	2.0	3.0	4.0	5.0	6.0	8.0	10.0	11.0	12.0	13.0	14.0	15.0	16.0	17.0	18.0	19.0	20.0

- Except for proposals that are awarded 0 or ¥2,000 and over, the evaluation ratio should be 50 percent receiving ¥500 and 50 percent receiving ¥1,000.
- Proposals that are not yet implemented are awarded either 0 or ¥500.

Creative Idea Evaluation Score Table

Benefit A

	0	1	2	3	4	5	6	7	8	9	10	11	12	13	14	15	16	17	18	19	20
Cost reduction (10,000s of yen/month)	0	<1.5	1.5	3	5.5	8	12	16	24	28	35	42	50	58	67	76	86	96	109	121	150 or more
Personnel reduction (number of persons)	no benefit												1				2				3 or more
Equipment investment reduction (10,000s of yen/month)	0	<1.5	1.5	3	5.5	8	12	16	24	28	35	42	50	58	67	76	86	96	109	121	150 or more
Labor-hour reduction (hours/month)	no benefit	1	10	30	50	70	100	130	160	200	250	300 or more									
Labor hour/personnel reduction (hours/month)	no benefit	1	55	110 or more																	

Benefit B

	0	1	2	3	4	5
Space saved (m²)	less than prescribed	100 exterior / 50 interior / 25 office	200 exterior / 100 interior / 50 office	300 exterior / 150 interior / 75 office	400 exterior / 200 interior / 100 office	500 exterior / 250 interior / 125 office
Safety		safer than before	safely maintained without extra effort	extra safety precautions taken to prevent trouble / careless accidents prevented	safety maintained mechanically (without human attention)	safely maintained in any kind of situation
Hygiene (environmental conditions)	no efficiency	environment improved, operation became easier	improved to the extent that it is not unpleasant; operations that cause fatigue are eliminated	troublesome environment improved; unnatural posture eliminated	workplace environment made more pleasant; stressful operations that had to be done in half-shifts are eliminated	created a superior environment that did not exist before; environment was improved or operations eliminated to a degree surpassing ordinary standards
Quality (excluding quantitative)	no benefit	product quality maintained or improved	occurrence of defects eliminated	defects eliminated; checks no longer necessary	quality and reliability improved; inspection eliminated	product value increased; company image improved
Other		slightly significant benefit	fairly significant benefit	significant benefit		extraordinary benefit
Adaptability	none	can be used within section	can be used extensively within division	can be used for same type of processing both at own factory and at other factories (suppliers)	can be widely used throughout the whole company, including diverse types of processing	wide range of applicability, both for whole company and for suppliers
Creativity	none	good because hints from others were applied	applicable and feasible; quite creative	excellent idea and means of implementing it, rather creative (can be submitted as an implementable new suggestion)	excellent idea and means of implementing it; very creative (patent application possible)	excellent idea and means of implementing it; extraordinarily creative (patent application possible)
Originality	none	good originality because of hints from others	significant observation of troublesome problems	good observation of neglected daily problem	excellent idea for solving major problem left untouched for a long time	extraordinary idea for dealing with major problem noticed by no one else for a long time
Effort	none	made efforts	worked hard to implement; made fairly strong efforts	worked hard for a long time to implement; made rather strong efforts	worked very hard and made very strong efforts to overcome all problems involving implementation	hard work and effort at an extraordinary level in overcoming adverse circumstances

- Work demerits (percentage reduction for suggestions related to one's own job)
- Demerits for line employees with technical ability

Subject	Suggestions made by foremen and group leaders	Suggestions made by general employees with technical ability related to improving their jobs	Joint suggestions made by foremen and group leaders together with general employees with technical ability, related to improving their jobs	+	Involving administrative and technical workers in implementation / Worker received advice	Involving administrative and technical workers in implementation / Worker received cooperation or assistance
%	10%	20%	20%		10%	20%

Demerits for administrative and technical staff

Subject	Suggestion substantially related to own job	Suggestion somewhat related to own job	Suggestion almost entirely related to own job
%	30-40%	20%	50% or more

Originally the standards were such that all unimplemented proposals would receive zero yen, but because of various circumstances within and outside the company, the ¥500 award was instituted as a relief measure in special cases. Thus the review standards were adjusted to reflect the attitudes and feelings of the proposal writers.

It should be noted that qualitative effect was the real aim of these standards, as one might expect from a mature proposal system such as that used by Toyota. Much can be learned in this respect from an examination of this sheet.

SIMPLE STANDARDS AND SIMPLE PROPOSAL FORMS

The chart on page 149 shows the evaluation standards used at Kanegafu Chemical Industries, based in Kashima. These standards apply to proposals in classes 8 through 6 (the lowest-ranking proposals, entitled to award amounts of up to ¥1,000); more detailed standards must be considered for proposals in classes 5 (a bonus amount of ¥2,000 to ¥3,000) through 1.

In the past the company used a more complicated method to calculate the awards, but many people felt that the evaluation standards were ambiguous and hard to understand. Once the standards were revised and simplified, people stopped complaining about ambiguity.

Particularly noteworthy is the creation of a category called "problem identification proposals." These suggestions are not thought out all the way to their solution; rather, they simply identify and alert others to problems. This makes it possible for employees who just point out problems to become involved in proposal activity. It also flushes out deep-rooted problems, raises the level of consciousness with respect to such problems, and helps educate people about proposal activity.

Evaluation Criteria for Improvement Proposals
(Kanegafuchi Chemical Industries Co., Ltd.)

1. Important evaluation aspects and content of the proposal

Effect	Improved productivity, better efficiency, lower cost, improved safety/hygiene/ quality, etc., the extent to which production will be influenced by this contribution. Also take into account related expenses of the company.
Originality and creativity	Degree of ingenuity and originality of the idea
Effort	The amount of effort required for implementation

2. Quick decision evaluation criteria (class 6 or higher)

(1) Evaluation chart

Rank	Evaluation	Not bad	Good	Very good
Proposal Type	Evaluation criteria	△	○	◎
Implemented proposal	Effect and degree of creative thinking, amount of effort	Class 8 (¥200)	Class 7 (¥500)	Class 6 (¥1,000 – for higher awards see special chart)
Unimplemented proposal	Anticipated effect and quality of proposal	Participation bonus (¥100)	Class 8 (¥200)	Class 7 (¥500)
Problem detection	The extent of the problem and the extent of its examination	Participation bonus (¥100)	Class 8 (¥200)	Class 7 (¥500)

(2) Scale of the problem

Possibility of implementation / Investment (yen)	Work team can solve	Solution possible within section	Solution requires other sections
100,000 or less	Rank A		
100,000 – 1,000,000		Rank B	
1,000,000 or more			Rank C

Note: This system ranks proposals in classes 1 through 8, with 1 being the highest level and 8 the lowest level above a basic participation award. This form permits quick evaluation of the lower classes (6, 7, and 8).

Simple Proposal Forms from Two Companies

Proposal forms used by Minolta Camera and Mazda are illustrated on pages 151 through 156.

In addition to a full-length proposal form, Minolta Camera also uses a brief half-sheet memo proposal form. This makes it easier to write simple descriptions of ideas on improving things employees have noticed.

Mazda also has two types of proposal forms. Form A is a regular proposal form, and form B provides space for writing down five proposals. This design for writing several proposals into one form helps keep the records in one ledger. It also saves time and labor since each name and code must be entered just once. This is a rational method for accounting and administrative procedures.

A multi-proposal form also invites supervisors to ask, "How about one or two more proposals to fill up the form?" This is an effective way of getting employees to take another look at the workplace and see what problems lie buried under the surface.

Since people have a tendency to overlook and neglect small problems, a simple proposal form can be used to identify such problems and encourage workers to improve the situation. The final effect of this method is probably very good indeed. At the moment quite a few companies are using two different types of proposal forms, and most of them use the simplified form as one of them.

But problem awareness is only one of the effects of proposal forms. They also promote on-the-job training through proposal activity. Once an efficient proposal system is in place, these simple proposal forms can be utilized effectively. If such a system is not in place, simplified forms will not be useful. Remember that many companies get a large number of proposals using full-scale forms.

Minolta Short Form

"ATTACK 2,000 CASES"

Date: _____

What I'd like to improve: _____

Name: _____

Problem areas

1) dangerous
2) causes poor quality
3) difficult
4) broken
5) narrow
6) high, low
7) long, short
8) out of order
9) requires too much effort
10) waste of time
11) sloppy
12) easily breaks down
13) heavy, light
14) other ( )

My idea:

Use, don't use	Implemented	Examined	Don't use
Opinion			

DO YOU HAVE ANY PROBLEMS?

Date: _____

The area I would like to improve is: _____

Name: _____

Situation: _____

Problem area: _____

Improvement proposal: _____

Please draw a simple picture:
(before improvement)

(improvement idea)

Use, don't use	Implemented	Examined	Don't use
Opinion			

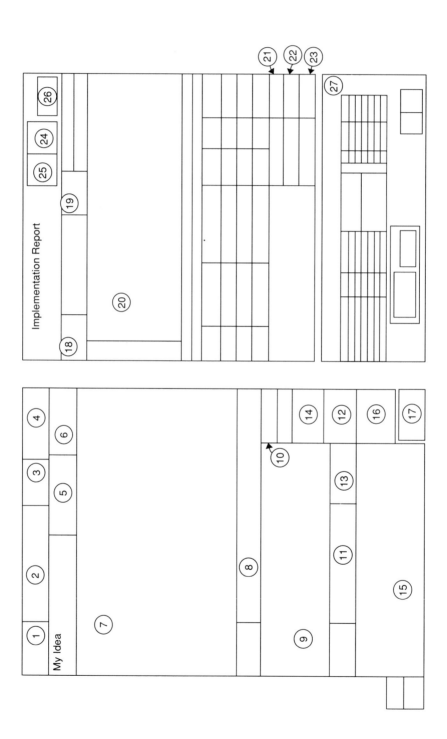

Minolta Full-length Form

(1) Proposal No.

(2) Subject, ideas

(3) Section No.

(4) Name

(5) Date

(6) Department abbreviation

(7) Proposal/drawing

(8) Effect, anticipated savings

(9) Description of effect

(10) Types of Teian

(11) Range of application

(12) Supervisor's stamp

(13) Result of first review

(14) Section head's stamp

(15) Evaluator's comments

(16) Section head's stamp

(17) Proposal writer's signature

(18) Implementation level/Basis for calculation

(19) Implementation period (dates)

(20) Report on implementation/calculation effect

(21) Total kaizen effect (6 months)

(22) Expense (6 months)

(23) Net savings

(24) Supervisor's stamp

(25) Section head's stamp

(26) Proposal writer's signature

(27) Second review chart (grade and award levels)

Mazda Kaizen Proposal Sheet (A)

Employee number

	Please route to the section chief	Date of request	Requesting department	
		Request no.	Cost control department	Approval
Request for review of implemented proposals.	Opinion of the implementation office	1. Use proposal 2. Do not use (reason) 3. Already reviewed 4. Other		
	Plant department: Telephone:	Circle: General / Technical / Department head / Assistant manager / General manager	Rejected	Reference
Notification of evaluation results.	Name of case		Incentive bonus	Prize bonus
	Employee name/no.	Commendation no.	Number of proposers	Class	Award amount
					Office stamp
				Review date

Remember to fill in the information inside the heavy line

Plant department		Proposal submission date	
Employee names/numbers			Commendation no.
Name of case	Target department no.		
Procedure before improvement	Proposed improvement		
Simple drawing			

1. Proposal only   2. Implemented proposal (date: _____)
(circle one)

Effect in monthly savings	(expenses) ¥/month	(number of plants) time/month	
	Prize bonus (¥3,000 -)	incentive bonus (¥150)	prize bonus (¥1,000)	reference (0)	rejected (0)

Review category	Dept. head		Section mgr.
	Supervisor		Team leader

Official opinion

Circle applicable category:
1. Use and implement proposal (expected time of implementation: _____)
2. Under investigation
3. Currently impossible to obtain results quickly — application postponed, not implemented
4. Passed on to the department in question.
   Department manager:

Corporate office	¥/month	Time/month

Mazda Kaizen Proposal Sheet (B)	Fill in only the part applicable to incentive bonuses for implemented proposals; do not fill in for other proposals.				Date:	Departmental review	
						Reviewer	
Workplace code Supervisor:	Worksite:					Super-visor	Dept. head
Where the proposal applies (location)	Imple-mentation date	Subject (what)	Reason (why)	Description of implementation (how did I change it?)	◯		
Employee name/number:					Bonus	No Award	
Workplace: Station:	Part no. and what has been improved				Factory number		
Employee name/number:					Bonus	No Award	
Workplace: Station:	Part no. and what has been improved				Factory number		
Employee name/number:					Bonus	No Award	
Workplace: Station:	Part no. and what has been improved				Factory number		
Employee name/number:					Bonus	No Award	
Workplace: Station:	Part no. and what has been improved				Factory number		
Employee name/number:					Bonus	No Award	
Workplace: Station:	Part no. and what has been improved				Factory number		

1. Please fill in this sheet only for incentive bonuses that apply to implemented proposals. Do not fill in this sheet for other proposals.	Department and office stamp	
2. Please fill in for five submitted proposals.		
3. Please fill in items inside the thick line clearly and accurately. Use the same form for all proposals.		

A Comparison with Old Regulations

The figure on pages 158-159 provides a comparison of old and revised proposal regulations and criteria at Nichii Co., Ltd. It is particularly enlightening to juxtapose the portions of the regulations that state the purpose of the proposal activities.

The purpose under the new regulations has just three parts. They are concise and clear. By contrast, the old regulations have a very elaborate statement of purpose. It is solemn and obliging, filling up a sizable chapter. One might expect such a solemn formulation to bring forth excellent proposals, but it had the opposite effect. Proposal activity was in poor shape. Once simple and intelligible regulations were adopted, proposal activity improved; this was reflected in the results of the service and sales department.

Of course, you cannot transform the proposal system by simply rewriting a chapter of the rules. You must first change what is behind the written chapter, namely, the way problems are tackled and the general conditions. Real results come only through changes made in actual conditions, never through superficial changes and ploys to attract customers. A change in conditions, however, soon will be visible on the surface.

Nichii's list of new evaluation criteria is also interesting. Instead of a formula for calculation or a matrix for prompt decisions, it uses an even more uncomplicated and straightforward method. This revised version presents a sharp contrast to the complex standards used in the service or production departments of large companies. This should be a source of inspiration for those who believe they must create complicated formulas.

Simple imitations of the forms shown here will probably not fulfill the forms' proper function in every company. The reason for this is that each company is at a different stage of development, with differing conditions.

Old Regulations (paragraph 2): Purpose

> The purpose of the incentive system is to gather original and ingenious innovative opinions and conclusions from all the employees with respect to environmental, economical, technological, and other aspects of our activity, which will prove beneficial to management and which will at the same time serve to strengthen the positive interest and understanding of our employees in our common problems, as well as serve the purpose of improving voluntary participation and cooperation with the management of our company. In short, our aim is to create a pleasant working environment through real improvements brought about by proposal activity, which emphasizes the importance of the human factor in creating a good working atmosphere (based on genuine respect for people).

B. Old Regulations

Evaluation Factors	Principal Review Items and Evaluation Points															
Effect (40)	Very significant				Considerable				Small				Not significant			
	40	38	36	34	30	28	26	24	20	18	16	14	10	6	4	0
Originality (25)	Highly novel and creative				Quite original, offering a wide sphere of application				Can be creatively applied with some help; creative when widely applicable				Similar examples elsewhere; not very insightful, but has reference value			
	25		23		20	18		16	14	12	10	8	6	4	2	0
Effort (20)	Required a great deal of effort				Required quite a bit of effort				Required some effort				A lucky strike, very little effort			
	20		18		16	14		12	10	8		6	4		2	0
Possibility of implementation (15)	Can be implemented immediately				Requires a preparation period				Still some room for improvement and more thinking				Will require further study; hard to tell if proposal has much future			
	15		12		10		8		6		4		2		0	

New Regulations (paragraph 1): Purpose

> The purpose of the proposal system defined by these regulations is:
> 1. To encourage creativity and inventiveness of our employees, since this is beneficial to the management of our business.
> 2. To improve voluntary participation of our employees in management and planning activities and to create a better working environment.
> 3. To contribute to further development and improvements in the organizational structure of our company.

A. New Regulations: Award Criteria

Class	Bonus Type	Bonus Amount	Criteria
First award	Challenge	¥300	The effect is not significant, but the considerable effort required by the proposal should be recognized and acknowledged by a bonus.
	Hint	¥500	The effect is small, but the proposal can be implemented immediately and this fact should be acknowledged.
	Idea	¥1,000	It is a great idea and some effect is expected, although the proposal must be studied; all of this should be acknowledged.
	Best	¥3,000	Considerable effect; the proposal is very creative and it can be implemented right away
Second award	Copper	¥10,000	
	Silver	¥20,000	
	Gold	¥30,000	

Before drawing up a proposal form, a company should take account of actual circumstances at the company and analyze the purpose of the form. It is especially important to ask the following questions:

1. What is the most important problem that our company is facing right now?
2. At what stage of development are we now?
3. What kind of mechanism do we need, and what strategy will make this mechanism work?

Although examples from other companies represent an excellent reference source, each company must come up with its own version and its own strategy. Any type of form adopted by any company has only temporary value and should be changed at some point. Its usefulness applies only to a certain point of development, nothing more and nothing less. As the conditions of the development activity and its priorities change, it is only natural for the corresponding mechanisms and the strategies that make these mechanisms work to change as well. Proposal activity is like a living organism. It should never be treated as a permanent fixture.

PART FOUR

Examples of Kaizen Teian Promotion Activities

Kaizen teian activities are introduced and promoted in a variety of ways. Since each workplace has a different experience with this activity, it may be instructive to examine some actual examples of proposal activity. The four case studies that follow were compiled from proposal activity reports that were presented at annual meetings convened every year by JHRA in several regions of Japan.

The accounts in this chapter describe personal experiences and examples of creative improvement proposals by several outstanding innovators. These contributions are presented in the form of cartoons, through which their original and ingenious ideas were recorded for the company newspapers. This chapter also highlights some of the responses of meeting participants to the improvement accounts.

The companies studied in this section are

Honda Motor Co., Ltd.
Nichii Co., Ltd.
Tokai Bank Co., Ltd.
Shizuoka South Post Office

A Dream of Unlimited Possibilities, or Learning from Rice Balls

(Honda Motor Co., Ltd., Sayama Plant)
by Masanori Ino

The Honda Sayama plant is a specialized assembly plant where everyone works hard to build Honda cars. The primary models produced here are the Regent Accord and the Prelude.

I didn't start working for Honda until I was 52 years old. My main job at that time was to fit steel sheets on the body to keep out the elements. I was also working at a sealing plant where we made sure that rust wouldn't affect the edges of car parts.

One day the supervisor approached me.

"Hey, Ino!"

"What is it?"

"Your trunk is a goldfish tank!"

"Huh? What are you talking about? How could there be goldfish in the trunk?"

"You dodo, I don't mean there are really goldfish swimming in the trunk. What I meant was that five cars are *no good* because water is leaking in. Five new cars — that would be ¥10,000,000 (approximately $66,000 at ¥150/$1)."

"¥10,000,000!!"

"You have to do better! Never mind the money; we must make cars that will please our customers, cars that we would want to drive ourselves."

At the time, I didn't understand very well what making improvement proposals was all about, and I didn't expect much from kaizen activity. It was a concept I didn't really comprehend.

I was later transferred to work in a water processing station. At the end of the first month, we had a visitor, a guy who was promoting improvement proposals. He said that each worker should make three proposals. I didn't think I could come up with more than two, so I went to talk with our group leader toward the end of the shift.

"Can you tell me what improvement proposals are really about?"

"Come here a moment."

"Okay," I said.

"Do you notice something here?"

"The floor is pretty dirty; I'll clean it up."

A little while later I came back to him: "I'm done cleaning, can I go now?"

"You call this cleaned up? It's filthy!"

"But I washed it and got it nice and clean. How come it's dirty again?" I couldn't figure it out.

"Well, you have to do something, and do it today."

So I poured water on the floor and cleaned it one more time. When I was done, I noticed that a little bit of sludge was leaking from the ground packing of the pump. And as it spilled out of the pump joint, it made a mess all over the floor because the drainage hose was clogged.

I explained everything to the group leader and we had a conversation about what to do. Maybe we could figure out a proposal for the best solution if we gave it some thought. I decided to take one more look and think about what to do.

Honda has a slogan called the Three Principles of Actuality: *Never stop thinking about the ACTUAL situation of*

ACTUAL objects at your ACTUAL place of work. I applied this by taking a good look at the workplace situation, a really thorough inspection.

I discovered that the ground packing was loose, so I tightened it up again. The joint outlet was too narrow and the hose was too long. I made a larger opening, then shortened and reattached the hose. I cut a channel so the sludge from the hose would drain properly, and covered it with a steel plate for safety. Finally, I noted the changes on the inspection tag and on the clipboard log sheet.

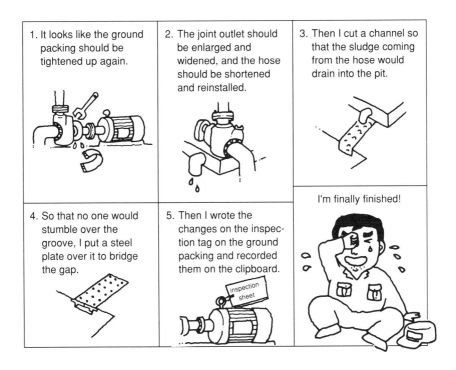

1. It looks like the ground packing should be tightened up again.

2. The joint outlet should be enlarged and widened, and the hose should be shortened and reinstalled.

3. Then I cut a channel so that the sludge coming from the hose would drain into the pit.

4. So that no one would stumble over the groove, I put a steel plate over it to bridge the gap.

5. Then I wrote the changes on the inspection tag on the ground packing and recorded them on the clipboard.

I'm finally finished!

Even small improvements add up and build confidence. Before you know it, even a worker that no one takes seriously can mature and suggest innovative proposals.

COMMUNICATION AND PERSEVERANCE

As we become more experienced in making improvement proposals, we begin to understand how often we become victims of our own dogmatic attitudes and preconceptions. Even if we get a good result, by neglecting good communication with our colleagues at work, we may blow our chances of implementing more kaizen proposals in the future. It's not possible without reliable communication.

Since the workplace is sometimes organized in several shifts, problems can also arise when an improvement proposal is implemented during one shift without being discussed by the people on the next shift. When the next shift arrives for work, people complain about the change and argue about its necessity. I have also experienced how difficult it is to get colleagues to understand what I was trying to do. In particular, my group leader got very upset when he felt my explanation was unsatisfactory. I often asked myself, when our opinions collided, "Why is this guy so thick? How can I make him see things my way?"

Once, when I was a member of the kaizen proposal promotion committee for our group, proposals were so scarce that we made a "rule" to implement and submit each month all the proposals received within the month. This was not only my job; each member of the group was also supposed to implement some proposals. They would say things like "I've already proposed three," and "I had a total of five; that's it for me," or "I'm saving those last two proposals for next month."

I hounded them for proposals. I wouldn't take no for an answer; they nicknamed me the "proposal demon." My operating principle was that if you apply enough force, you can wring something out!

As I soon found out, you can't squeeze innovative ideas out of unwilling people. There had to be a new approach.

A LESSON FROM RICE BALLS

It was a real agony to me, trying to persuade members of my team to come up with something. I was at a loss for a solution, so I made plans to go hiking with my wife, hoping for some diversion from these problems. I wanted to take along rice balls, a traditional "portable" Japanese food, for our lunch. My wife is not Japanese, and I was trying to help her get used to Japanese customs.

The day before our hike, I showed her how to roll sticky rice around the filling, and explained to her how to prepare pickled plums and fish eggs for the middle.

The next day, I got up bright and early, ready for the hike following day. I was excited and went to the kitchen for a little taste of the rice balls. With great anticipation, I bit into one. It was a shock to the mouth to find, not fish eggs, but roast beef. A Japanese would never think to put roast beef inside a rice ball. Once I got used to it, though, it was not bad.

This event destroyed forever my preconceptions about what should be inside a rice ball lunch. My wife's concept of lunch was anything that a hungry person would like to eat, with ingredients selected at will. While munching on our tradition-shattering rice balls, I couldn't help thinking: if we want to foster creative thinking, we have to throw away our preconceived notions of what improvement activity is all about and of the ways to introduce more concrete improvement proposals.

Our habits, things that we tend to do every day without much thinking, may seem perfectly natural to us, especially when they relate to our work. But isn't it true that this kind of thinking also tends to suppress each person's unique qualities so that they are not creatively developed?

The inspiration I drew from the rice ball incident gave me another idea for putting the proposal activity in a more concrete form. If you look at rice balls from a distance, you can't smell what is inside — there is no telling what it could be.

It finally dawned on me that the function of improvement proposals is not only to identify areas where problems are obvious, but also to dig out hidden problems, buried deep under the surface.

IMPROVEMENT THROUGH COOPERATION
WITH ANOTHER SECTION

As part of a total overhaul of the production technology at our Sayama plant, we were able to satisfy the sewage regulations using one less water purification facility. We thought we might find something resourceful to do with it, rather than leaving it idle.

One idea was that, if a catalytic oxidation tank, which requires few operators, was shared between the chemical synthesis section and the equipment control section, it would eliminate the need for more purification facilities. Thus we could purify the water more efficiently and save energy. We had to run many tests, analyze the quality of water, and compare literature on the subject. Often we were groping in the dark in our joint meetings, but after six months we finally stabilized the quality of the water discharged from the sewer system. Because the new design also saved energy, we managed to reduce the cost of energy required for chemical synthesis by ¥280,000 a month, while the share of equipment management costs was reduced by ¥250,000, for a total savings of ¥530,000 (approximately $3,500 at ¥150/$1).

Measures to Improve Water Quality at Sayama Sewage Treatment Plant

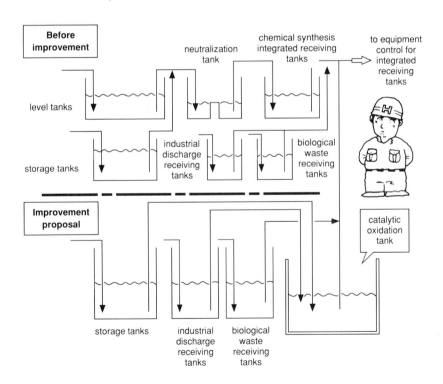

WINNING HONDA'S KAIZEN PROPOSAL PRIZE AFTER 10 YEARS WITH THE COMPANY

My winning of Honda's Prize for Kaizen Proposals came not just through my own effort. I was fortunate to have the cooperation of my supervisors, my coworkers, and last but not least, my wife. I had to push the section manager a bit to get a written proposal from him, but for the first time I got two proposals. This made me very happy and was quite an encouragement at the time. It also took some doing to get the group leader to decide on a budget for implemented proposals, but eventually that happened, too.

I learned a thing or two from the incident with the rice balls. Because I received the Honda Prize, I was sent on a study tour to the United States. On the trip over, I thought back over those 10 years and silently thanked all the people who had helped me along the way.

Personal Conversations — A Key to Promoting Kaizen Proposal Activity

(Nichii Co., Hirakata Store)
by Shigetugu Kuroki

"You want *me* to do it?"

The year was 1982. The store manager had asked me to take responsibility for the kaizen proposal activities at our store. A request from the store manager is in effect an order that must be obeyed.

But writing proposals is my weak point. When he asked me to do this, I wondered how on earth I could provide guidance to others when I didn't know anything about proposals myself. I had never felt so awkward.

We had a suggestion system in place before, but with no special department to handle it, no one was doing much. We had to intensify our kaizen proposal activities and make the system work. Because propsals didn't seem to be forthcoming, the store manager put me in charge of promoting them.

My job is merchandise management and control at the Hirakata store of the Nichii company. I work in the department that handles the records for received and forwarded merchandise. The Hirakata store, opened in 1968, has a 23,000-square-foot selling area. Our sales are primarily clothing and underwear for men, women, and children, and accessories and toiletries. The store employs 44 people, 56 percent of whom are part-timers.

Our employees are good, friendly people. I told the store manager I'd do my best to encourage improvement proposals.

The initial results were not encouraging. That first year, employees wrote only 122 proposals, against a target of 456. That was 2.4 proposals per employee, only 26.7 percent of the target number. The employees just weren't participating.

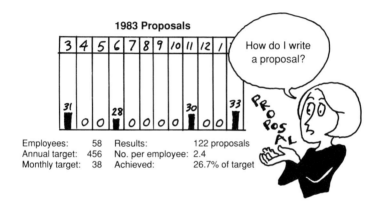

No matter how hard I tried, I still got no results. I put together a diagram explaining proposal activity so that people could read it and start learning about proposals. We started giving bonus awards for proposals, but it still didn't catch on. People didn't know how to write proposals and were embarrassed to show them to their supervisors.

Everyone had a reason why he or she shouldn't have to submit improvement ideas. The part-time employees were particularly difficult to approach. They felt we should leave them alone and ask only the full-time employees for ideas.

At the beginning of 1983, I made set up these guidelines:

• Quantity before quality.
• Describe in your own words the problems you have noticed, without worrying about the economic effect.

I put each department manager in charge of distributing proposal forms to the leaders of the QC circles.

The next year's numbers came in looking great. We had proposals every month and met our target by 101 percent; 52 employees wrote 462 proposals, an average of 8 proposals per employee.

At first I was very pleased, but as I continued to read proposals I discovered that most of them were complaints or requests — what this or that person would like to have, what is wrong with things, and what was bothering people. It seemed that people who did want to submit serious proposals were afraid that they would displease their managers by questioning their management methods. Unfortunately, the workplace culture was such that the managers were not enthusiastic about suggestions to improve management, and were extremely irritated when such suggestions went over their heads to the proposal reviewers.

Two groups began to form — those who submitted proposals and those who didn't submit any. Some people loved to make proposals, but many felt that they were not creative and didn't have any good ideas. How could I change their minds?

In 1984, I formed a new proposal implementation committee and set the following policies to improve proposal activities:

- Post proposals that received participation or merit awards, along with the department manager's comments. This will help employees learn how to identify problem areas and write about them.
- Remember to thank employees for their ideas when you review their proposals.

One of the proposals that year was an improvement over the daily procedure of moving the cash register stands from the front of the store into the office at the end of the day. This was heavy work, even for strong employees. The improvement idea was to put casters on the stand so that it rolls easily into the office — something anyone can do.

Another example involved privacy for customers using the rest room. The customer rest rooms used to be clearly visible from the salesroom; this was not in very good taste and therefore undesirable. The proposal was to install a partition that hid the stalls from the open entrance.

Unfortunately, it still took a lot of persistence to get an idea like this implemented. When employees ask what has become of their proposals, we are often forced to answer, "Oh, yes, we're looking into it right now." The employee who had this idea wanted to see it implemented quickly, so rather than getting the same old answer, she actually proposed the same thing five different times before it was implemented.

When we started proposal activities in 1985, I made a resolution to visit personally anyone who did not submit a proposal and help him or her write one. The dialogue often went something like this:

"I would like to ask you for a proposal."

"Oh, I'm just not good at writing — I don't think I could handle making proposals!"

"We're not asking you for something difficult and complicated. All we want to know is what you think about problems you see every day where you work."

"When I'm about to write something, I'm never sure I'll be able to express what I mean. It's hard for me, you know?"

"Well, why don't you tell me about your ideas, and I'll write them down for you?"

When some people even then couldn't come up with a proposal, we gave them a topic to think about (called the target topic). In this way we motivated our employees to participate in the activity.

In 1985, we had results that were truly gratifying. In the first ten months, 44 employees wrote 567 proposals, achieving 102.7 percent of the annual target. This averaged out to 12.3 proposals per employee. Participation improved to 100 percent.

My boss, the store manager, commended me on these results, recognizing that the active approach I had adopted had considerably improved the overall attitude toward proposal-writing in the company.

Some lessons learned include:

- Express your appreciation to the employee for his or her suggestion when you review and comment on proposals each submits.
- Try to make comments in a way that will not upset the person submitting the idea — put yourself in his or her shoes.
- When commenting on unacceptable proposals, focus on the possibility for future proposals with comments like, "We are hoping to receive new proposals from you."
- Make comments only after personally visiting the place referred to in the proposal and experiencing the actual situation.

Improving Banking
Procedures with Kaizen

(Tokai Bank Co., Ltd., Kanayama District Center)
by Yuriko Konishi, Takiko Torii, Naoko Tazawa,
Natsuko Ooda, and Kiyomi Uchijima

The Kanayama district center was established in May 1983. During my time there, the center was characterized by its lively atmosphere. The force behind this lively atmosphere was our improvement activity.

HOW WE IMPROVED PROPOSAL ACTIVITY

Proposal activity was forced on us by our supervisors when the center opened. We had no clue as to what they wanted us to submit every day.

People had various reasons for not submitting proposals. Some said, "I don't know how to write; it's too difficult for me." Others felt that people would not understand what they meant. Many simply felt "too shy."

The working conditions at the center were hard on us. But we were not interested in the proposal system and never submitted kaizen proposals. After all, we had been taught to do our jobs in strict accordance with procedures; how could we possibly make changes in the way we worked?

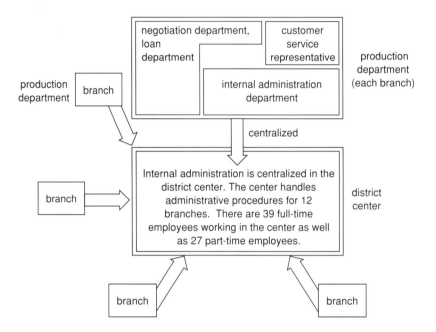

Many people were transferred to this center from various branches. In talking with them, we discovered that the branches don't all perform the work the same way. Then the center director clarified that the policy was to change the procedural rules when they were not working well. Our center's new approach:

- Let's devise more pleasant methods without neglecting anything.
- We must get rid of fixed ideas.
- We learn about things only by trying them out.

From July 1983 through December 1986, our center had 1,537 proposals submitted. Of these, 845 were implemented, a rate of 55 percent.

It was very encouraging that every proposal we made, no matter how insignificant it seemed, was seriously considered.

Two of the proposals we submitted were selected by the main office for bonus awards for excellence. The money we received for those proposals was used to buy a small memento for each person. The illustrations show some of the proposals we implemented.

Our kaizen proposals are simple ideas, unlike some industrial inventions and patents in various fields. They represent a positive and forward-looking effort of the employees. That is why even a seemingly insignificant proposal should be treated with respect.

Our district center has recently attracted so much attention that our organizational model has become a leading model for all the district centers of our company.

Summary of Proposals

Office standardization	4 proposals	• standardized ledger entries • a more rational levying of service fees • preparing operation manuals • a more rational way to transfer customer slips
Waste elimination	4 proposals	• a new system for using rubber stamps • using a pushcart • an improved system for using the bookbinder • color coded cards for storage baskets
Improved work environment Total: 13 proposals	5 proposals	• a hanging box for customer slips • boxes for storing customer slips and rubber stamps • a hanging notice board for important messages • a revolving office procedure chart • relocating wastebaskets and modifying the trash can lid.

Proposals per Employee

(source: JHRA, 1986)

	Per employee/per year
Financial industry	5.5 proposals
This center, previous year	14.0 proposals
New annual target	20.0 proposals

Practical Example 1: Identical Bookkeeping Method for Ledger Entries

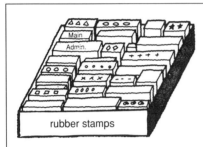

rubber stamps

Before Improvement

The bookkeeping method involved using the rubber stamps of each branch. Some stamps were bigger, some smaller, and there were 30 of them in the box. An entry in one line had to be stamped with several different stamps.

Good Idea | Each line should be stamped with only 1 rubber stamp.

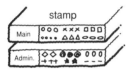

stamp

One stamp combines the branch name with several different symbols used in the "Summary" column. The person making the entry simply circles the appropriate symbols.

Manager			
Date	Branch	Summary	Loan
	Main	ooo ×××⬜⬜⬜ •••• △△△ ⊙⊙⊙	
	Admin.	⊙⊙ ●●● ooo ++++ ★♣ - - -	

After Improvement

The number of rubber stamps was reduced from 30 to 6. This made the ledger easier to read since the same method was used for everything.

Effect

Anyone could make entries in the ledger at the same speed and using the same method, irrespective of who was doing it and which branch he or she was from.

Identical bookkeeping method for ledger entries

Since we all work in the same bank, we thought that every branch would be using the same ledger, but the content was completely different in each branch. It took a lot of time just to find the right rubber stamp for a branch that one was not used to dealing with, which was a waste of time and money.

We had the idea to use only one rubber stamp for each line. In this way, we could have a set of 6 kinds of rubber stamps, and we could use them to make a uniform system of ledger entries for all the branches.

This was our first step toward a unified administrative system at our bank.

Practical Example 2: Changing the System of Notifying Customers about Incurred Service Fees

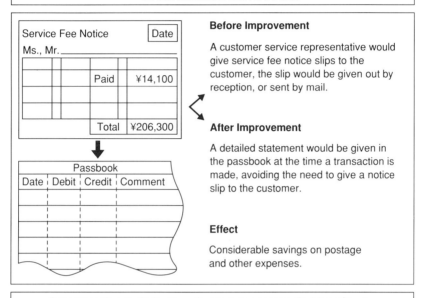

Service Fee Notice			Date
Ms., Mr. _____			
		Paid	¥14,100
		Total	¥206,300

Passbook			
Date	Debit	Credit	Comment

Before Improvement

A customer service representative would give service fee notice slips to the customer, the slip would be given out by reception, or sent by mail.

After Improvement

A detailed statement would be given in the passbook at the time a transaction is made, avoiding the need to give a notice slip to the customer.

Effect

Considerable savings on postage and other expenses.

Practical Example 3: New System for Using Rubber Stamps

Before Improvement

Rubber stamps that were in use and those that were not in use were all kept in a box on the desk.

After Improvement

Stamps that were not being used were collected and arranged in one location, and the rules were changed so that people had to check before ordering new stamps.

Changing the System of Service Fee Notices

Example 2 shows how important it is to examine the things we take for granted and discuss ideas with each other. Since the customer is the most important person in the bank, we decided to implement this proposal after seeing that our customers accepted it.

New System for Using Rubber Stamps

This proposal emphasizes that the most important thing in the drawers and cupboards is space. It's a waste to clog that space with extra boxes of stamps that are not needed.

Practical Example 4: A Hanging Rack for Customer Slips

The processed customer slips take up space on the desk and cause confusion. If we could get rid of the box, we'd have a lot more desk space.

processed slips

unprocessed slips

stamps

Next day

Let's submit a proposal to apply this to the data processing area.

If everyone pitched the customer slips into a basket as they were processed (like playing basketball), the boxes on the desks could be eliminated.

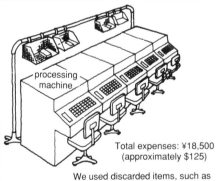

processing machine

Total expenses: ¥18,500 (approximately $125)

We used discarded items, such as chair bases, and had to buy only the pipe for the rod.

Effect

- We can now use the entire desk space.
- The system also helps keep different slips from being mixed together.

Before Improvement

The box for storage of customer slips used to take up space on top.

After Improvement

We attached a rod to hold hanging racks over the stations, where we could toss the processed customer slips.

Cheers!

We received a bonus award for this proposal and used it to celebrate our success.

Practical Example 5: Improvements to the Customer Slip and Rubber Stamp Storage Boxes

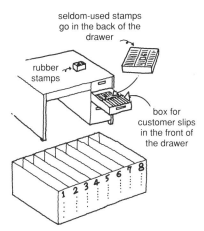

seldom-used stamps go in the back of the drawer

rubber stamps

box for customer slips in the front of the drawer

We created a manual explaining how to use the box and wrote the instructions on a piece of cardboard.

Before Improvement

Because we used to put the customer slips and rubber stamps into the big box placed on top of the desk, in no logical order, only the person desig- nated to do this job could use the slips and the stamps. When anyone else had to do the job, it was difficult to find everything. The desk was also crowded.

After Improvement

We created a universal form for every- one to use and a uniform system for storing them.

Effect

No matter who sat at the desk, every- one now knew what was where. We designed the arrangement so that it would also be convenient for opera- tions in other departments.

Practical Example 6: A Hanging Bulletin Board for Communicating Important News

Before Improvement

When we had to inform employees about important things, we used to stick notices on a notice board, write them on the blackboard, and post them on the walls. Even so, many people never got the news. (Even when we announced things over the speaker system, some people were on the phone and didn't hear it.)

After Improvement

We created a "bulletin board" of cardboard and suspended it from a string in front of the office door so that a person could not walk in without hitting it.

Some people have to be hit on the head before they get it!

Effect

People hate it when it hits them, but they always notice what it says. Now we have a reliable method for informing everyone.

As office standardization is progressing, not only are the divisions between different jobs dissolving, but we are now having to figure out how to do jobs that never existed before.

Practical Example 7: Preparing Office Standardization Manuals

Before Improvement

We had to read massive collections of office procedures and learn from oral instructions. There were some jobs for which we had no rules at all.

After Improvement

We prepared procedural manuals.

Effect

Anyone can now do any job. We have prepared almost 200 different types of manuals, and we are still working on new ones.

It is no longer necessary to memorize which procedure is used with which operation. When we are under time pressure, we can now assign responsibilities to different people, since we are using standardized stamps to process the documents. This has certainly speeded up document handling at our office. Because of these changes, we can now tell who is in charge of which operation at any given moment, which is a relief to us.

Practical Example 8: A Rotating Chart Board for Office Procedures

Procedural Chart

helps
people
remember
certain
steps

Before Improvement

We used to keep a procedural check chart on top of the desk, but it was always in the way and no one in our group wanted to use it.

After Improvement

Taking advantage of free space overhead, we designed and made a chart board that rotated. This way it was easy for anyone to see the board.

Effect

The check chart is no longer in the way and is easy for anyone to see. We linked it with our new customer slips storage box, manuals, and other parts of the processing system, thus creating useful tools of office standardization.

Practical Example 9: Using a Pushcart to Transport Records

Before Improvement Every day, to bring records for bookbinding, we had to carry some 50 to 70 cases of customer slips.

After Improvement We installed fencing mesh on a general purpose pushcart so that we could safely lock the enclosure. This saved a lot of unnecessary carrying.

Every morning and evening we had to haul those cases.

Practical Example 10: Changing the Layout and Improving a Bookbinder for Customer Slips

We use a bookbinding machine to consolidate customer slips.

bookbinder

slips

Before Improvement

We had to gather customer slips and bring each bundle separately to the bookbinder, put them inside, switch it on, and wait two minutes until the binding was finished.

Improvement Idea

• We put together a turntable platform that made it possible to turn the bookbinder around.
• Then we placed the bookbinder between our tables so that 4 people could use it in this location and could do other things while they waited for the binding to be completed.

Effect

Now we can use the machine right at our desks because we can reach it by hand. Binding time was reduced by 1 minute per 1 bundle of customer slips. In this way we saved about 1 hour of lost time each day.

Practical Example 11: Color Coding Customer Slip Storage Baskets

Here it is!

there are 50 - 70 boxes

Before Improvement

We used to arrange the bundles of customer slips on end in the baskets, so we couldn't tell the branch name and date unless we took them out one by one.

After Improvement

We cut thick cardboard labels, using a different color for each branch, coded them with numbers from 1 to 31 (for the date), and placed them on the bundles of customer slips.

Effect

• Office standardization (elimination of time loss)
• Fewer errors

Practical Example 12: Changing the Position of the Wastebasket and Designing a Wastebasket Container

It should never happen, but sometimes we would lose customer slips this way, which would always create a great stir. Let's face it, if you put the wastebasket right next to the desk, there is a good chance that important customer slips will end up there.

This led to the following proposal . . .

Before Improvement

We used to keep the wastebasket next to the desk. Since it had no lid, we would simply empty everything into it.

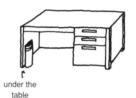

under the table

lots of space

Even if you drop something important, you will probably notice it.

After Improvement

Staff members put their baskets under the table so that they would be conscious of throwing away only things they really wanted to get rid of. We fitted the lids on the big trash cans with small openings so that employees have to feed papers through them one by one. This way we can check every time what we are throwing out.

I'll check one more time to make sure I'm not throwing out something important.

Effect

Prevents accidental disposal of customer slips.

prevents accidents

Practical Example 13: Sharing the Work to Eliminate Unnecessary Transfer Trips

EXCHANGE DEPT.

You know, Ms. Obara, if we did this processing in the deposit department, we wouldn't have to transport each customer slip one by one to the exchange department for this purpose. What do you think?

You're absolutely right — that's a great idea.

This conversation was the first step in an effort to simplify communication within the company.

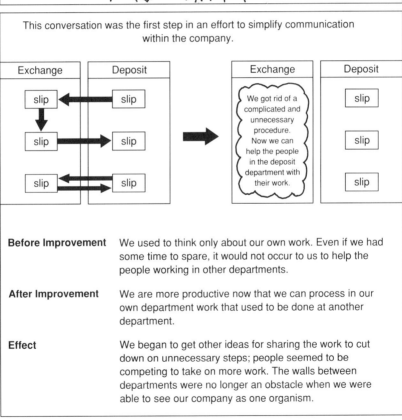

Before Improvement   We used to think only about our own work. Even if we had some time to spare, it would not occur to us to help the people working in other departments.

After Improvement   We are more productive now that we can process in our own department work that used to be done at another department.

Effect   We began to get other ideas for sharing the work to cut down on unnecessary steps; people seemed to be competing to take on more work. The walls between departments were no longer an obstacle when we were able to see our company as one organism.

Rising to the Challenge
of Problems

(Shizuoka South Post Office)
by Osamu Yamazaki

The Shizuoka South Post Office, where I work, is located in the southern part of Shizuoka City, which is blessed with the cool and pleasant climate for which Mt. Fuji is famous. Our office also serves as a regional post office center for transportation of mail and parcels. Night operations play an important role in regional post offices as a crucial element for speeding delivery the next day.

Although I joined the post office 20 years ago, my first opportunity to rise to the challenge of improvement proposals came in 1983. At the time, actually, I was known to all as the office grouch. Complaints, grievances, and dissatisfaction were what everyone always expected from me, and usually got.

One day, my boss, Mr. A, said to me that people who complain all the time never change anything. "You will never be a real leader," he said. "All you can do is criticize — and your criticism is too harsh. The least you can do is write a kaizen proposal!"

These statements shook me up a bit, because I take my work seriously. After Mr. A said this, I decided that instead of constantly criticizing, I would think about improvement proposals.

In 1984, I was promoted to team leader, in charge of four or five people. I vowed to do a good job. Shortly after my appointment, Mr. S, a freshman at the Postal Services Training Institute, was assigned to my group. He surprised me by turning in kaizen proposals, which, for him, were easy to make. Despite my seniority, I learned a lot from him about proposal activity.

In July of that year, a new manager joined the branch. He commended me for my efforts in encouraging proposal activity. Encouragement from the managers is an important stimulation for proposal activity; that's a fact. During this manager's time in office, I was fortunate to get a lot of encouragement from him.

After a year, I was transferred to the Postal Services Training Institute in Nagoya, where I was trained for a new position. There I learned that one of the main duties of managers is to provide guidance to those working below them. One day the director addressed us about kaizen and said, "The *biggest* problem is when you believe that you have *no* problem in your department!"

These words made a big impression on me. I recognized the challenge in solving problems. I decided that when I returned to the Shizuoka Post Office I would find them and solve them. Let me tell you about some of the problems we identified and how we solved them.

IMPROVEMENT EXAMPLES

Even at our best, we can never sort more than 2,000 letters per hour. Today just about every large post office is equipped with an automated letter-sorting machine. With this machine it is possible to process up to 40,000 letters per hour. Since it can run nonstop, it does a job that would ordinarily take 20 people.

Although it happens very rarely, sometimes a letter will be dropped on the floor. Machine sorting has been severely criticized because of this problem. There is a lot of resistance to automating the sorting operation, and managers felt they had to back up the machine with manual labor. This problem, however, can be solved by mounting a barrier that prevents the letters from falling out of the machine.

Another problem is letters getting caught in the machine and jamming it in several different places. We developed a number of countermeasures to deal with this problem. We also studied the problem of mail cart bumpers that wore out too fast. These kaizen proposals are described in the illustrations.

In April 1985, I was nominated as the top employee in proposal promotion activity. When you work as hard as you can, you will in the end create something that benefits everyone.

Whenever I found my job difficult, I always remembered the advice of my former manager, Mr. A. Through his advice, I became a leader in improvement proposals.

The most important thing is to ask yourself:

• What kind of proposal would fix this?
• What is the problem?
• Are other improvements possible?

The role of a leading worker who promotes improvement proposals is to vanquish negative expressions like, "I don't

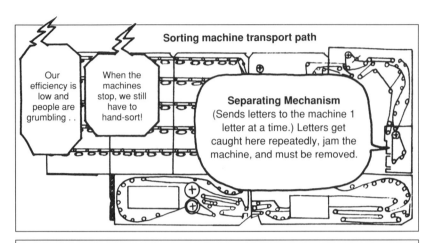

Sorting machine transport path

Our efficiency is low and people are grumbling . .

When the machines stop, we still have to hand-sort!

Separating Mechanism
(Sends letters to the machine 1 letter at a time.) Letters get caught here repeatedly, jam the machine, and must be removed.

Before Improvement

① Not all letters fit into the collecting box; larger letters wouldn't go all the way in.

② Letters got caught on the top edge of the plastic board.

③ They also caught on the clasp of the plastic board.

④ Some letters easily got caught in the upper part of the collecting box.

Jamming of the separating mechanism

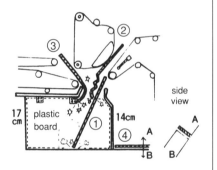

side view

17 cm   plastic board   14cm

After Improvement

① The collecting box was enlarged and deepened; all letters now enter the box smoothly.

② The top of the plastic board was cut diagonally, which made it harder for letters to catch on it.

③ The position of the clasp on the plastic board was moved out of the way.

④ The inner part of the collecting box was beveled, which made it easier to spot letters.

Effect

Jamming was eliminated.

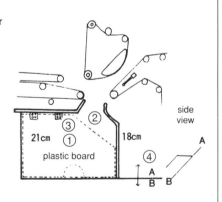

side view

21cm   ③   ②

① 18cm

plastic board   ④

A   A   B   B

understand this" and "I can't do that." To create a well-function-ing improvement proposal system, you have to be in close con-tact with submitted proposals. To build participation and increase the number of proposals, the manager has to stop throwing away proposals that are "no good" and instead teach people how to turn these ideas into real proposals.

Another important element of a good system is obtaining the backing of your superiors. Even when many people are will-ing to participate in proposal activity, there is nothing you can do if your superiors will not listen to what the innovators have to say. Through the backing of my manager and the director with respect to organizing proposal activity, I was able to put together a well-functioning system for improvement proposals.

People compete with each other even when they work dur-ing the day within the same department. At night they will dream about becoming the office manager or the company pres-ident. I think that this competitive spirit can be channeled to produce improvement proposals.

The number of proposals grew every year (see chart). We asked each employee to identify and improve at least seven problems a year.

We are just beginning to rise to the challenge of problems. Meeting the needs of the customers and providing good service is possible only through the cooperative effort of all employees.

Number of Proposals Submitted	
1982	53
1983	108
1984	1,334
1985	2,660
1986	2,924
1987	Target: 7 or more per person

Postscript

This book is a compilation of a revised and reconstructed collection of special articles dealing with proposal activity. The articles were published in *Ingenuity and Inventions*, a monthly magazine dedicated to the kaizen teian movement.

In the past, publicity about proposal activity came mostly from progressive manufacturing corporations. Today, however, proposal activity can be found in a wide range of industries and business areas. Accordingly, the literature and know-how has extended into new areas, as businesses try to respond to the needs of readers and customers for cross-currents of available information. The need for current information has burgeoned because it is no longer possible to simply imitate the examples of others.

The topic of this book extends beyond the limits of ordinary reporting, in which the reporter would interview kaizen teian promoters and proposal writers, then write up stories. We felt the need to organize study groups and meetings where opinions, information, and documents were exchanged with people on the promotional committees of many different companies. Through this process, the concepts underlying implemented kaizen teian activities were clarified. This is a basic philosophy, common to all companies that are successfully managing improvement proposal systems.

The contents of this book have been exposed to examination and critique following their publication in *Ingenuity and Invention* articles or their use in seminars and consulting. This revision of the suggestion system based on the implemented proposal philosophy and on new attitudes — reflects practical and verifiable results achieved in the workplace. The value of this book results from the input from managers involved in promoting proposal activity, and from supervisors who collected data and assisted our cooperative exchanges. We would like to express our deep gratitude for their invaluable assistance with this book.

Proposal activity is something that can be practiced at any company and by every worker. There is no perfect blueprint for this activity that can be copied by everyone. Even when several workplaces use similar proposal forms, the actual activities are often diverse. Each company must develop its own model. Like other companywide activities, proposal activity has its own stages of development. Kaizen teian needs continual development if it is to grow.

USING STRATEGY TO TEACH KAIZEN

We close the book with a summary of the range of managerial approaches to developing kaizen teian activities. There are five basic approaches to leadership that have very different effects on the success and growth of improvement proposal activities.

- *Aggressive:* Some managers have a style that is aggressive, angry, and autocratic. If kaizen activities do not produce immediate results, their approach would be to eliminate the activities. With this outlook, kaizen activities won't get far.

- *Complaining:* Only a notch above this kind of belligerence is a manager who sees that nothing is happening and complains about it. This type of person thinks there is nothing to be done and so does nothing to encourage participation and creative improvements.
- *Patient:* A third type of manager waits for people to show interest before stepping in to help them. This approach is more progressive than complaining about things, but still doesn't get the best results.
- *Generous:* One approach that's better than merely waiting is to "prime the pump" by writing proposals on behalf of one's employees.
- *Strategic:* The best solution is a strategic approach. The manager with this approach is an optimist who works for long-term results. He or she makes a continued effort to teach the principles of kaizen so that employees can make their own kaizen. This may take longer, but it is the best approach for successful kaizen activities.

We hope that this book and the other volumes of this series will help managers find their own positive approaches to promote kaizen activities and help their employees develop creative solutions in the workplace.

Index

COMPLETE LIST OF TITLES FROM PRODUCTIVITY PRESS

Akao, Yoji (ed.). **Hoshin Kanri: Policy Deployment for Successful TQM**
ISBN 0-915299-57-7 / 1991 / 256 pages / $49.95 / order code HOSHIN-B201

Akao, Yoji (ed.). **Quality Function Deployment: Integrating Customer Requirements into Product Design**
ISBN 0-915299-41-0 / 1990 / 387 pages / $ 75.00 / order code QFD-B201

Akiyama, Kaneo. **Function Analysis: Systematic Improvement of Quality and Performance**
ISBN 0-915299-81-X / 1991 / 288 pages / $59.95 / order code FA-B201

Asaka, Tetsuichi and Kazuo Ozeki (eds.). **Handbook of Quality Tools: The Japanese Approach**
ISBN 0-915299-45-3 / 1990 / 336 pages / $59.95 / order code HQT-B201

Belohlav, James A. **Championship Management: An Action Model for High Performance**
ISBN 0-915299-76-3 / 1990 / 265 pages / $29.95 / order code CHAMPS-B201

Birkholz, Charles and Jim Villella. **The Battle to Stay Competitive: Changing the Traditional Workplace**
ISBN 0-915299-96-8 / 1991 / 110 pages / paper / $9.95 /order code BATTLE-B201

Christopher, William F. **Productivity Measurement Handbook**
ISBN 0-915299-05-4 / 1985 / 680 pages / $137.95 / order code PMH-B201

D'Egidio, Franco. **The Service Era: Leadership in a Global Environment**
ISBN 0-915299-68-2 / 1990 / 165 pages / $29.95 / order code SERA-B201

Ford, Henry. **Today and Tomorrow**
ISBN 0-915299-36-4 / 1988 / 286 pages / $24.95 / order code FORD-B201

Fukuda, Ryuji. **CEDAC: A Tool for Continuous Systematic Improvement**
ISBN 0-915299-26-7 / 1990 / 144 pages / $49.95 / order code CEDAC-B201

Fukuda, Ryuji. **Managerial Engineering: Techniques for Improving Quality and Productivity in the Workplace** (rev.)
ISBN 0-915299-09-7 / 1986 / 208 pages / $39.95 / order code ME-B201

Gotoh, Fumio. **Equipment Planning for TPM: Maintenance Prevention Design**
ISBN 0-915299-77-1 / 1991 / 320 pages / $ 75.00 / order code ETPM-B201

Greif, Michel. **The Visual Factory: Building Participation Through Shared Information**
ISBN 0-915299-67-4 / 1991 / 320 pages / $49.95 / order code VFAC-B201

Hatakeyama, Yoshio. **Manager Revolution! A Guide to Survival in Today's Changing Workplace**
ISBN 0-915299-10-0 / 1986 / 208 pages / $24.95 / order code MREV-B201

Hirano, Hiroyuki. **JIT Factory Revolution: A Pictorial Guide to Factory Design of the Future**
ISBN 0-915299-44-5 / 1989 / 227 pages / $49.95 / order code JITFAC-B201

Hirano, Hiroyuki. **JIT Implementation Manual: The Complete Guide to Just-In-Time Manufacturing**
ISBN 0-915299-66-6 / 1990 / 1006 pages / $2500.00 / order code HIRJIT-B201

Horovitz, Jacques. **Winning Ways: Achieving Zero-Defect Service**
ISBN 0-915299-78-X / 1990 / 165 pages / $24.95 / order code WWAYS-B201

Ishiwata, Junichi. **IE for the Shop Floor: Productivity Through Process Analysis**
ISBN 0-915299-82-8 / 1991 / 208 pages / $39.95 / order code SHOPF1-B201

Japan Human Relations Association (ed.). **The Idea Book: Improvement Through TEI (Total Employee Involvement)**
ISBN 0-915299-22-4 / 1988 / 232 pages / $49.95 / order code IDEA-B201

Japan Human Relations Association (ed.). **The Service Industry Idea Book: Employee Involvement in Retail and Office Improvement**
ISBN 0-915299-65-8 / 1991 / 294 pages / $49.95 / order code SIDEA-B201

Japan Management Association (ed.). **Kanban and Just-In-Time at Toyota: Management Begins at the Workplace** (rev.), Translated by David J. Lu
ISBN 0-915299-48-8 / 1989 / 224 pages / $36.50 / order code KAN-B201

Japan Management Association and Constance E. Dyer. **The Canon Production System: Creative Involvement of the Total Workforce**
ISBN 0-915299-06-2 / 1987 / 251 pages / $36.95 / order code CAN-B201

Jones, Karen (ed.). **The Best of TEI: Current Perspectives on Total Employee Involvement**
ISBN 0-915299-63-1 / 1989 / 502 pages / $175.00 / order code TEI-B201

JUSE. **TQC Solutions: The 14-Step Process**
ISBN 0-915299-79-8 / 1991 / 416 pages / 2 volumes / $120.00 / order code TQCS-B201

Kanatsu, Takashi. **TQC for Accounting: A New Role in Companywide Improvement**
ISBN 0-915299-73-9 / 1991 / 244 pages / $45.00 / order code TQCA-B201

Karatsu, Hajime. **Tough Words For American Industry**
ISBN 0-915299-25-9 / 1988 / 178 pages / $24.95 / order code TOUGH-B201

Karatsu, Hajime. **TQC Wisdom of Japan: Managing for Total Quality Control**, Translated by David J. Lu
ISBN 0-915299-18-6 / 1988 / 136 pages / $34.95 / order code WISD-B201

Kato, Kenichiro. **I.E. for the Shop Floor: Productivity Through Motion Study**
ISBN 1-56327-000-5 / 1991 / 224 pages / $39.95 / order code SHOPF2-B201

Kaydos, Will. **Measuring, Managing, and Maximizing Performance**
ISBN 0-915299- 98-4 / 1991 / 304 pages / $34.95 / order code MMMP-B201

Kobayashi, Iwao. **20 Keys to Workplace Improvement**
ISBN 0-915299-61-5 / 1990 / 264 pages / $34.95 / order code 20KEYS-B201

Liebling, Henry E. **Handbook for Personal Productivity**
ISBN 0-915299-94-1 / 1989 / 128 pages / $9.00 / order code PP-B201

Lu, David J. **Inside Corporate Japan: The Art of Fumble-Free Management**
ISBN 0-915299-16-X / 1987 / 278 pages / $24.95 / order code ICJ-B201

Maskell, Brian H. **Performance Measurement for World Class Manufacturing: A Model for American Companies**
ISBN 0-915299-99-2 / 1991 / 448 pages / $49.95 / order code PERFM-B201

Merli, Giorgio. **Co-makership: The New Supply Strategy for Manufacturers**
ISBN 0915299-84-4 / 1991 / 224 pages / $39.95 / order code COMAKE-B201

Maurer, Rick. **Caught in the Middle: A Leadership Guide for Partnership in the Workplace**
ISBN 1-56327-004-8 / 1991 / 272 pages / $24.95 / order code CAUGHT-B201

Productivity Press, Inc., Dept. B201, P.O. Box 3007, Cambridge, MA 02140 1-800-274-9911

Merli, Giorgio. **Total Manufacturing Management: Production Organization for the 1990s**
ISBN 0-915299-58-5 / 1990 / 224 pages / $39.95 / order code TMM-B201

Mizuno, Shigeru (ed.). **Management for Quality Improvement: The 7 New QC Tools**
ISBN 0-915299-29-1 / 1988 / 324 pages / $59.95 / order code 7QC

Monden, Yasuhiro and Michiharu Sakurai (eds.). **Japanese Management Accounting: A World Class Approach to Profit Management**
ISBN 0-915299-50-X / 1990 / 568 pages / $59.95 / order code JMACT-B201

Nachi-Fujikoshi (ed.). **Training for TPM: A Manufacturing Success Story**
ISBN 0-915299-34-8 / 1990 / 272 pages / $59.95 / order code CTPM-B201

Nakajima, Seiichi. **Introduction to TPM: Total Productive Maintenance**
ISBN 0-915299-23-2 / 1988 / 149 pages / $45.00 / order code ITPM-B201

Nakajima, Seiichi. **TPM Development Program: Implementing Total Productive Maintenance**
ISBN 0-915299-37-2 / 1989 / 428 pages / $85.00 / order code DTPM-B201

Nikkan Kogyo Shimbun, Ltd./Factory Magazine (ed.). **Poka-yoke: Improving Product Quality by Preventing Defects**
ISBN 0-915299-31-3 / 1989 / 288 pages / $59.95 / order code IPOKA-B201

Nikkan Kogyo Shimbun/Esme McTighe (ed.). **Factory Management Notebook Series: Autonomation/Automation**
ISBN 0-0-56327-002-1 / 1991 / 200 pages / $125.00 / order code N1-AA-B201

Nikkan Kogyo Shimbun/Esme McTighe (ed.). **Factory Management Notebook Series: Mixed Model Production**
ISBN 0-915299-97-6 / 1991 / 184 pages / $125.00 / order code N1-MM-B201

Nikkan Kogyo Shimbun/Esme McTighe (ed.). **Factory Management Notebook Series: Total Productive Maintenance**
ISBN 1-56327-003-X / 1991 / 184 pages / $125.00 / order code N1-TPM-B201

Nikkan Kogyo Shimbun/Esme McTighe (ed.). **Factory Management Notebook Series: Visual Control Systems**
ISBN 0-915299-54-2 / 1991 / 194 pages / $125.00 / order code N1-VCS-B201

Ohno, Taiichi. **Toyota Production System: Beyond Large-Scale Production**
ISBN 0-915299-14-3 / 1988 / 162 pages / $39.95 / order code OTPS-B201

Ohno, Taiichi. **Workplace Management**
ISBN 0-915299-19-4 / 1988 / 165 pages / $34.95 / order code WPM-B201

Ohno, Taiichi and Setsuo Mito. **Just-In-Time for Today and Tomorrow**
ISBN 0-915299-20-8 / 1988 / 208 pages / $34.95 / order code OMJIT-B201

Perigord, Michel. **Achieving Total Quality Management: A Program for Action**
ISBN 0-915299-60-7 / 1991 / 384 pages / $45.00 / order code ACHTQM-B201

Psarouthakis, John. **Better Makes Us Best**
ISBN 0-915299-56-9 / 1989 / 112 pages / $16.95 / order code BMUB-B201

Robinson, Alan. **Continuous Improvement in Operations: A Systematic Approach to Waste Reduction**
ISBN 0-915299-51-8 / 1991 / 416 pages / $34.95 / order code ROB2-C-B201

Robson, Ross (ed.). **The Quality and Productivity Equation: American Corporate Strategies for the 1990s**
ISBN 0-915299-71-2 / 1990 / 558 pages / $29.95 / order code QPE-B201

Productivity Press, Inc., Dept. B201, P.O. Box 3007, Cambridge, MA 02140 1-800-274-9911

SANNO Management Development Research Center (ed.). **Vision Management: Translating Strategy into Action**
ISBN: 0-915299-80-1 / 1991 / 208 pages / $29.95 / order code VISM-B201

Sekine, Kenichi. **One-Piece Flow: Cell Design for Transforming the Production Process**
ISBN 0-915299-33-X / 1991 / 320 pages / $75.00 / order code 1PIECE-B201

Shetty, Y.K and Vernon M. Buehler (eds.). **Competing Through Productivity and Quality**
ISBN 0-915299-43-7 / 1989 / 576 pages / $39.95 / order code COMP-B201

Shingo, Shigeo. **Non-Stock Production: The Shingo System for Continuous Improvement**
ISBN 0-915299-30-5 / 1988 / 480 pages / $75.00 / order code NON-B201

Shingo, Shigeo. **A Revolution In Manufacturing: The SMED System**, Translated by Andrew P. Dillon
ISBN 0-915299-03-8 / 1985 / 383 pages / $70.00 / order code SMED-B201

Shingo, Shigeo. **The Sayings of Shigeo Shingo: Key Strategies for Plant Improvement**, Translated by Andrew P. Dillon
ISBN 0-915299-15-1 / 1987 / 208 pages / $39.95 / order code SAY-B201

Shingo, Shigeo. **A Study of the Toyota Production System from an Industrial Engineering Viewpoint**
ISBN 0-915299-17-8 / 1989 / 293 pages / $39.95 / order code STREV-B201

Shingo, Shigeo. **Zero Quality Control: Source Inspection and the Poka-yoke System**,Translated by Andrew P. Dillon
ISBN 0-915299-07-0 / 1986 / 328 pages / $70.00 / order code ZQC-B201

Shinohara, Isao (ed.). **New Production System: JIT Crossing Industry Boundaries**
ISBN 0-915299-21-6 / 1988 / 224 pages / $34.95 / order code NPS-B201

Sugiyama, Tomo. **The Improvement Book: Creating the Problem-Free Workplace**
ISBN 0-915299-47-X / 1989 / 236 pages / $49.95 / order code IB-B201

Suzue, Toshio and Akira Kohdate. **Variety Reduction Program (VRP): A Production Strategy for Product Diversification**
ISBN 0-915299-32-1 / 1990 / 164 pages / $59.95 / order code VRP-B201

Tateisi, Kazuma. **The Eternal Venture Spirit: An Executive's Practical Philosophy**
ISBN 0-915299-55-0 / 1989 / 208 pages/ $19.95 / order code EVS-B201

Yasuda, Yuzo. **40 Years, 20 Million Ideas: The Toyota Suggestion System**
ISBN 0-915299-74-7 / 1991 / 210 pages / $39.95 / order code 4020-B201

Audio-Visual Programs

Japan Management Association. **Total Productive Maintenance: Maximizing Productivity and Quality**
ISBN 0-915299-46-1 / 167 slides / 1989 / $749.00 / order code STPM-B201
ISBN 0-915299-49-6 / 2 videos / 1989 / $749.00 / order code VTPM-B201

Shingo, Shigeo. **The SMED System**, Translated by Andrew P. Dillon
ISBN 0-915299-11-9 / 181 slides / 1986 / $749.00 / order code S5-B201
ISBN 0-915299-27-5 / 2 videos / 1987 / $749.00 / order code V5-B201

Productivity Press, Inc., Dept. B201, P.O. Box 3007, Cambridge, MA 02140 1-800-274-9911

Shingo, Shigeo. **The Poka-yoke System**, Translated by Andrew P. Dillon
ISBN 0-915299-13-5 / 235 slides / 1987 / $749.00 / order code S6-B201
ISBN 0-915299-28-3 / 2 videos / 1987 / $749.00 / order code V6-B201

Returns of AV programs willl be accepted for incorrect or damaged
shipments only.

TO ORDER: Write, phone, or fax Productivity Press, Dept. B201, P.O. Box
3007, Cambridge, MA 02140, phone 1-800-274-9911, fax 617-864-6286. Send
check or charge to your credit card (American Express, Visa, MasterCard
accepted).

U.S. ORDERS: Add $5 shipping for first book, $2 each additional for UPS
surface delivery. CT residents add 8% and MA residents 5% sales tax. For
each AV program that you order, add $5 for programs with 1 or 2 tapes, and
$12 for programs with 3 or more tapes.

INTERNATIONAL ORDERS: Write, phone, or fax for quote and indicate
shipping method desired. Pre-payment in U.S. dollars must accompany your
order (checks must be drawn on U.S. banks). When quote is returned with
payment, your order will be shipped promptly by the method requested.

NOTE: Prices subject to change without notice.